Thomas Hospital
Heatlh Resource Center

Surviving Post-Natal Depression

D0064531

of related interest

Child Development for Child Care and Protection Workers
Brigid Daniel, Sally Wassel and Robbie Gilligan
ISBN 1 85302 633 6

Parenting Teenagers
Bob Myers
ISBN 1 85302 366 3

Growth and Risk in Infancy
Stephen Briggs
ISBN 1 85302 398 1

Family Support
Direction from Diversity
Edited by John Canavan, Pat Dolan and John Pinkerton
ISBN 1 85302 850 9

Child Welfare Policy and Practice
Issues and Lessons Emerging from Current Research
Edited by Dorota Iwaniec and Malcolm Hill
ISBN 1 85302 812 6

Early Experience and the Life Path
Ann Clarke and Alan Clarke
ISBN 1 85302 858 4

Surviving Post-Natal Depression

At Home, No One Hears You Scream

Cara Aiken

Jessica Kingsley Publishers
London and Philadelphia

We gratefully acknowledge the kind permission of the *Association for Post-Natal Illness* for the reprinting of their leaflet in Chapter 13.

All rights reserved. No paragraph of this publication may be reproduced, copied or transmitted save with written permission of the Copyright Act 1956 (as amended), or under the terms of any licence permitting limited copying issued by the Copyright Licensing Agency, 33–34 Alfred Place, London WC1E 7DP. Any person who does any unauthorised act in relation to this publication may be liable to prosecution and civil claims for damages.

The right of Cara Aiken to be identified as author of this work has been asserted by her in accordance with the Copyright, Designs and Patents Act 1988.

First published in the United Kingdom in 2000 by
Jessica Kingsley Publishers Ltd
116 Pentonville Road
London N1 9JB, England
and
325 Chestnut Street,
Philadelphia, PA 19106, USA

www.jkp.com

Second impression 2001
Copyright ©2000 Cara Aiken

Library of Congress Cataloging in Publication Data
Aiken, Cara, 1964–
   Surviving post-natal depression : at home no one hears you scream / Cara Aiken
      p.   cm.
   Includes bibliographical references and index.
   ISBN 1 85302 861 4 (pbk : alk paper)
   1. Aiken, Cara, 1964-- Health. 2. Postpartum depression--Patients--Biography. 3.
Postnatal care--Psychological aspects. I. Title.

RG852.A36 2000
362.4'9876--dc21
[B]   00-030180

British Library Cataloguing in Publication Data
A CIP catalogue record for this book is available from the British Library

ISBN 1-85302-861-4

Printed and Bound in Great Britain by
Athenaeum Press, Gateshead, Tyne and Wear

Contents

Foreword

The writer of this book was full of life and fun until she stopped contraception in order to start a family. From that moment she suffered from a series of psychological complications – the strain of delayed conception, the grief of miscarriage, fears that her first baby (Georgina) would die in the womb, a distressing delay in bonding, prolonged postpartum depression, and (with her second baby Tasha) a tangle of family jealousies. She reacted to these experiences by reaching out to other mothers with postpartum illness, travelling far and wide to interview the many who responded to her research appeal. She selected nine with particularly graphic personal histories, and their stories are the substance of the book.

She has organized her work in an ingenious weave of biography and thematic analysis. Separate chapters deal with each mother's background, adjustment to the newborn, the loneliness of mothers, the full development of the illness, the father's response, recovery and achievement of contented motherhood, and the help received from friends, family and various agencies. This is the core of the book, but she has also recruited a fistful of experts with different perspectives, who give their own ideas about the cause and cure of post-natal illness. Their contributions are put into context by Cara's comments.

This book is a rich source of information. The style is fresh, informal, colloquial, with much verbatim quotation, so that one almost feels present at the interviews. Many mothers will find that it speaks directly to them.

At the same time, the professional can use the 'case histories' to apply his or her own ideas. I am particularly impressed that Cara has presented the variety of post-natal mental illness – not just 'the blues', post-natal depression and puerperal psychosis, but also bonding disorders, pathological anxiety and problems of anger with impulses to harm, kill or abandon the baby.

She has described a cross-section of help and hindrance provided by the social and medical services in this country, which boasts of leading the world in services for mothers. One mother (Veritee), a social worker herself, struggling with a baby who failed to thrive because of heart disease, received no effective paediatric help for her child, no psychiatric help for herself, and from the child protection team no support at all – but instead, threatening case conferences targeted at her alleged neglect.

This mother asked the question:

'Why does society fail to cope with this very common illness, PND?'

Perhaps professionals fail because they do not work as a team, and because they cannot understand what (in detail) is wrong with these mothers; once properly diagnosed, every single one of their problems could have been dealt with effectively and rapidly. Professionals, however, will often fail, because of unlimited demands and the complexity of medicine. In the long run, we need a partnership between professionals and sufferers. The best way of combating the common problem of postpartum mental illness is to ensure that mothers everywhere – from all walks of life and all social levels – have a knowledge of the psychological complications of childbearing. The distant goal is a psychologically educated public, and Cara's book will help to achieve this.

Professor Ian Brockington, MD, FRCP,
Professor of Psychiatry at the University of Birmingham

Professor Brockington is a leading authority in the field of post-natal illness. His interest in pregnancy-related illness began in 1975, when he worked on the mother and baby unit in Manchester. Since going to Birmingham in 1983, he has developed a community-based service, backed by a day hospital and in-patient unit at the Queen Elizabeth Psychiatric Hospital.

This now receives over five hundred referrals a year. The nine-bedded mother and baby unit admits 75 mothers a year. Professor Brockington was a founder (1980) and first President (1982–1984) of the Marce Society, and the founder (1993) and Chairman (1996) of the section on women's mental health of the World Psychiatric Association. He is the author of several books and numerous papers and research reports on the subject, culminating in the book *Motherhood and Mental Health*, published in 1996.

Foreword

I am delighted to have been asked to contribute to Cara Aiken's book on post-natal illness. Having suffered severely from this debilitating illness, I know just how frightening it can be.

My depression began a week after my son Matthew was born. Having been healthy, happy and excited about the baby during my pregnancy, I was shocked that this could happen to me. I had a very supportive husband, a beautiful home, no financial worries and a wonderful family around me. This illness can affect *anyone*. I had a nervous breakdown.

PNI is a major maternal illness and it is not your fault. You must not feel guilty and you must remember that you will get better with the correct treatment. Do not be afraid of anti-depressants, as they are not addictive. Do not worry or feel guilty if you experience a lack of emotion towards your family or child – this will return as you begin to recover. Talk to other women who have recovered from PNI and contact the organizations listed at the back of the book for further help and advice. Remember, it may take some time but you *will* recover.

It is very important for any woman suffering from symptoms of PNI to seek help immediately. There is a stigma attached to any form of mental illness and we must all help to remove that. Cara's book will help increase the awareness of post-natal illness and offer comfort to fellow-sufferers and their families.

Denise Welch, actress,
currently starring in 'Coronation Street' as Natalie

Preface

I love and cherish my children more than anything else in the world. Ask me now if I would have forgone having them, and the answer would most certainly be no. I am just honest and happy enough *now* to admit that the shock of having a child to love, care for, and turn my life completely upside down for, affected me enormously.

The early stages were a living nightmare – emotionally, physically and most of all mentally. I initially blamed my hormones, then the lack of sleep, then my dog, and I finally came to the conclusion, much to my horror and disgust, that *I was the one to blame all along*. Was I simply just not an 'earth mother' figure? Why, oh why, was I hating my new role? My friends had coped admirably, my sister was thoroughly ecstatic with her new baby boy, and the media had painted a beautiful image of mother smiling serenely at her bundle of joy. So why was I so filled with dread at the sudden responsibility? Why was I so resentful about my life changing so drastically overnight? And believe me, it did. The 40-week pregnancy should have prepared me for my forthcoming child. The hours spent reading 'new baby' books made me mistakenly feel that I could conquer motherhood standing on my head. But I couldn't and my life was most certainly different now. Why had no one prepared me for this sudden impact on my emotions?

The fantastic relationship I had once had with my husband developed into pure resentment. I'd scream at him and hate him. He could walk out of the front door each day – I couldn't. My beloved old dog cowered while I had aggressive rages. I'd kick cupboards, bang my fists into the wall and scream and scream. I wanted to be my dog – then I wouldn't have a baby to care for. And then I'd dissolve into floods of tears – non-stop tears which seemed to go on for an eternity. I felt so guilty, lonely and terribly ashamed. What was I doing to my baby, my husband, my life?

Everyone would be better off without me. I wanted to die – the only possible escape I could logically think of. Luckily my doctor had a better idea – a damn good psychiatrist and a long-term course of anti-depressant tablets! My mental and emotional condition had finally been diagnosed – post-natal depression. Something I knew little if nothing about.

Looking back through my childhood and teenage years I realized why I, and probably the majority of women, never knew any better. We are conditioned by society from a very young age to love and care for our dollies, dress them, feed them and change their lovely clean plastic bottoms – not to mention being able to hold them by the hair while we do this or to push a plastic dummy into their mouths to stop them from crying (if our mother has not already removed the batteries!), or finally, just to toss the doll aside once we have had enough. We are then bought a nice toy hoover, washing-machine, play kitchen, etc. and have no problem in fitting the playful chores that these items imply into the course of the day.

We get a bit older and admire those beautiful babies in their prams, who will usually be smiling sweetly at us children. We say a few goo-goos and ga-gas and *walk away*. We then grow up and hope, if not expect, to one day have a baby of our own to love and to care for.

There are of course some women who take to motherhood like a duck takes to water. They love every minute of it, and can wax lyrical for hours about the niceties of bringing up their children. Then there are the breed of mothers who find their new role in life very difficult indeed.

We knew about the sleepless nights, the crying baby and the nappy scenarios, but put this into practice along with the complications of getting on with a near normal lifestyle and the result is not quite what we previously imagined it to be. For many mothers, the first five years, until the child is settled in full-time school, are the most traumatic. It can be extremely difficult to cope with your daily routines, do the utmost for your child and still find time to love your husband, walk the dog, not to mention running a home.

Unfortunately, post-natal illness was never discussed during the ante-natal period. We were not prepared to deal with the unexpected and extremely frightening feelings which develop gradually after giving birth. At first you blame the negative thoughts and tiredness on the fact that you are so exhausted. But you are exhausted because you cannot sleep. You cannot sleep because you are suffering from depression. You are depressed because you have had a baby.

You feel guilty, isolated, lonely, confused and ashamed. Do you discuss these feelings? Most of us don't and won't. We suffer in silence. We do not believe that any other mother has felt this way. We are bad. Should not have had children. Will be punished for our thoughts and feelings.

The reality is that approximately one in ten mothers suffer from a form of post-natal illness. Common symptoms include depression; fatigue; sleeping difficulties; feelings of guilt (not fulfilling the expectations of motherhood); feelings of inadequacy; loss of appetite; irritability; acute anxiety; fear of being alone with baby; fear for baby's well-being; fear of 'cot death'; fear about own physical and mental health; clinging to someone for constant support; hostility towards partner or loved ones; unexplained tearfulness; loss of enjoyment and inability to laugh; not coping; panic attacks; feeling of isolation; lack of confidence; bad memory; night sweats; unexplained fear about everything; suicidal tendencies;

temptation to injure child; loss of libido; low self-esteem/self-image; numbness; paranoia; constant physical ailments; obsessive behavioural patterns; the fear of further pregnancies and of PND; lack of bonding with baby; false self-expectations; inability to concentrate; utter despair; feeling trapped; lack of enthusiasm.

If this hits a nerve with you, or sounds at all familiar, take comfort in the fact that this is something a lot of women feel when they struggle through the first few years of motherhood.

In my book, I aim to clear up a few of the misconceptions about motherhood, get rid of the guilt factor altogether, and keep you feeling good about your relationship with your children and your lives. It will make you aware of the negative and unfulfilled feelings that many other mothers have experienced, and may just help you to accept that you are certainly not a bad mum – just normal.

Acknowledgements

Almost harder than writing the book itself – I've so very many people to thank. My first massive 'thank you' has to go to my good friend Tessa Beck. Tessa, you have given me encouragement and support, and have constantly kept my enthusiasm alive when I've felt, many times, like giving up. You've been my proof-reader, adviser, editor and confidence-booster. You have given so much of yourself to me during the past five years and I will be for ever deeply grateful.

Second, I would like to thank my husband and best friend Roo. He has stood by me through my repeated episodes of deep depression and yet continued to love and support me through the writing of this book. Roo, like me, had his problems during the earlier stages of our children's lives, but has become the most fantastic father, with the warmest heart, filled with love and passion for our children. I love you Roo – you are most certainly my brightest star.

This book would not have been possible without my contributors – Rosemary, Julie, Jane, Gail, Veritee, Pippa, Sarah, Jenny and Laura. Each one of you has given so much of your time and emotions and I thank you all so very much. Let's hope that through our own experiences we can save many future mothers from the pain and suffering we endured.

Thank you to all the professionals who have worked so hard with their contributions – Dr Dormon, my three health visitors working for the East Hertfordshire NHS Trust, Pauline Maddinson, Ann Herreboudt and Clare Delpech. Extra-special thanks to Professor Ian Brockington for his input throughout my book, and for my wonderful foreword; a big thank you to Denise Welch too for her foreword. Dr Malcolm George, you've really excelled with your chapter – so many fathers get forgotten along the way. I pray that your contribution will change society's perception of PND.

Thank you to all my friends and family for your support and encouragement, and for putting up with the numerous times I have cancelled arrangements to work on the book. Here's hoping I'll be more reliable in the future!

Finally but most importantly I wish to thank my two beautiful daughters Georgina and Tasha. You have taught me so much – I still learn from you both the most important things in life, each and every day. You have filled my life with happiness. Without you this book would not have existed. I love you with all my heart and soul.

The Contract

Some people love their jobs. Some people thrive on their work. It consumes their minds, their lives, their world.

Some of us hate our jobs. We feel miserable at the prospect of our day ahead. Our stomachs churn the night before, especially after a blissful weekend off. Still, we can always hand in our notice and look for something more suitable and enjoyable.

But what if the 'job' is that of a mother? We know that we should be enjoying this job, but we don't. We took the job with false ideals – the reality never met up to our dreams. Our stomachs churn at night, *every* night, and every day. There are no weekends off. We cannot hand in our notice even though this job is not at all suitable or enjoyable. We have taken on a responsibility and must now learn to love this baby who has not just rented a cot and room here, but has become a permanent and demanding fixture.

The nappies, bottles, screaming and colic were not part of the contract, but we never read the small print.

Introduction

Having suffered from post-natal depression following the birth of both my children, I decided five years ago, when my second daughter Tasha was born, to keep a diary of my thoughts and feelings. My long-term intention was to write a book. I then took this intention one step further and began a public research appeal to identify other women who were suffering, or had previously suffered, from post-natal depression – or post-natal illness, as it is also called (the two terms are used interchangeably in this book).

As my project progressed, I was horrified to realize that there was very little, if any, help available for women suffering from post-natal depression. We were all fighting to keep sane, feeling totally isolated in our emotions, and seemingly too scared to ask for help. Although we perhaps appeared reasonably 'normal' to the outside world, once behind closed doors the depression emerged in full force. No one would, or could, possibly understand how we were feeling. If we admitted just how desperate we were feeling, would our child be taken into care? This appears to have been a very prominent thought in most of our minds, and one very strong reason for not speaking out.

Were we trying to prove to all those 'copers' that we could cope too? And why on earth were we unable to? Why were we so unhappy in our new motherhood role? Emotional wrecks? How could we possibly admit that we were failing when we were desperately fighting to succeed? Was there anyone else out there experiencing these very same thoughts and feelings? We didn't know.

The books we read during our ante-natal period painted a truly beautiful picture of motherhood. Why were we not prepared during this time for the possibility of post-natal depression? Perhaps we would have looked for the warning signs or even recognized them. But by the time you are so far down, you are too far down to talk about it. An endless tunnel of confusion, misery, self-doubt and emotional turmoil looms ahead.

Who do you turn to, where do you go, what do you do? First, you must realize that you are *not* alone. However you feel, there *are* other women out there feeling the very same way. I realize that this issue is not well publicized – my very reason for writing this book.

Its structure is easy to follow. It is written totally from the heart, in simple terms, for every woman who finds herself screaming after the birth of her child and doesn't know why. It consists of sixteen chapters, the first ten set out bio-graphically, starting with my own experience of post-natal depression, and followed by those of the nine other women who have kindly contributed their personal accounts of their illness to this book.

Chapter 11 is an analysis of these ten chapters which draws out the themes of the stories, observes the symptoms and circumstances, and generally summarizes the case studies.

Dr Malcolm George, of the Men's Studies Research Group, Department of Physiology, St Bartholomew's and Royal London Hospital Medical School, has constructed Chapter 12. He has studied closely the personal accounts of both the women and the men involved. His interest in depression and how it affects the male partner is discussed in great detail. I feel sure that his contribution will offer the family as a whole an invaluable understanding of this complex illness and give you, the reader, the confidence and comfort you may so desperately need. I am deeply grateful to him for the time and effort he has spent in making sense of a subject which even I, as the author of this book, thought I would for ever feel confused about.

Chapter 13 consists of some authoritative and extremely valuable contribu-tions from the professional sector. The remaining chapters are written by myself and the nine other contributors. Here we offer practical advice and our own con-clusions drawn from our personal experiences.

It is important to mention that, having interviewed a staggering number of women who had suffered from post-natal depression, I had to battle with myself over whose experiences to use. Every story was as important as the next, but they could not all be included. Therefore, I have made a selection which I feel reflects the circumstances of the 'average' woman. I hope that by doing this I will have given each reader the opportunity to identify with someone.

You will see that in the personal accounts every case contains a brief biography, giving you the opportunity to establish a 'relationship' with each person by offering you an insight into her life prior to, and following, the birth of her child or children. The stories progress into our initial feelings during the first couple of weeks at home with the baby – our reactions to the child and to our role as a mother.

We had all been through the pregnancy, experienced the 'girl or boy? factor', given much thought to what to name the baby, predicted the birth date, made decisions on pain relief, practised our breathing exercises and finally survived the labour and birth. FULL STOP. This is where the information stopped. It was then that we realized we had not been given a lesson on motherhood.

We go on to explain how the reality of having a baby lived up (or didn't) to the image created during the pregnancy – how having this child is a real and massive responsibility – how hard it is to learn to love and develop a relationship with the tiny 'stranger'.

The books we had previously read about motherhood could not have painted a more unreal picture. They were all textbooks, using a model child, which we all know do not truly exist. The illustrations depicted a round, rosy-cheeked baby happily gurgling, with its mother smiling lovingly at her bundle of joy. Not a red-faced, skinny, wrinkled screaming creature, its mother tearing out her hair and with tears spilling down her cheeks. Now I know why I, and many other mothers, felt 'abnormal'.

It becomes increasingly difficult when suffering from post-natal depression to accept this feeling of 'abnormality'. Life becomes harder still when the support of the health visitor, midwife and, to some extent, family begins to disappear. I think that it was at this point, in most of our cases, that we began to feel more than slightly lost. We were trying to understand why we did not feel as elated as the media predicted. We did not understand why we were feeling so emotionally vulnerable.

I hope that what I have written about my first couple of years of being a mum will give you a more truthful picture of how difficult and unfulfilling that time can be. I have told no lies. I felt ashamed and sad while writing down my feelings. Then I read and inserted the stories that follow mine. Each writer said that she too had felt sad and ashamed while she was writing for me. And then I gave each of them a copy of each other's stories to read. What a reaction!

Even though they each knew that they were ill during that time, they still thought that they had been alone in their thoughts and feelings. They too were relieved to see that this was definitely not the case. As the author of this book, I felt an overwhelming relief as I inserted each story, one by one, into my manuscript. I had interviewed these women and heard their stories. Emotionally, I had lived their lives. Now it is all here to see – in black and white – the evidence that we had all suffered from the very same distorted thought patterns, had all been through hell – *alone*.

I felt further relief when I realized that I was not the only one who had experienced feelings of depression and doubt until my children individually reached the age of two. With each new stage of the baby's life came different problems. It seemed as if, each time I took one step forward, I would then take two steps back. There was nothing to suggest that things would ever improve. I did little to help myself. I accepted that life with a baby was an unhappy life and could not admit this to a 'professional', or anyone else for that matter, for a very long time. When I finally did admit this, I got better – just as everyone else in this book did.

Thankfully, post-natal depression over the years has become a much more recognized and accepted illness. If one doctor is not sympathetic, you will find the next one probably will be.

Although, because of the simple layout, this book can be dipped in and out of, I strongly recommend that you read it through and follow the stories as they unfold. I feel sure that you will identify with someone. Let these accounts of our illness give you the courage and confidence to ask for the help you may need.

Having spoken to literally hundreds of women and many experts, I discovered that there is apparently no conclusive evidence as to what causes the illness, or why some women suffer from it and others do not. In Chapter 15 I have revealed my own opinion as to why some women are affected by post-natal illness. It may well appear controversial, but it is what I have concluded from my research – this subject has never been honestly tackled and it's about time that it was.

I hope that you will find this book helpful and enjoyable, but above all I want it to give you the courage to keep on fighting, and to prove to you that there is a very bright light at the end of the tunnel.

Cara

I had been happily married to Roo for five years. We had a good social life, wonderful holidays, financial stability, a beautiful home, and both of us had secure jobs. Our relationship was filled with lots of fun and apart from loving each other deeply, above all else, we were great friends.

Our mutual friends were now having children, and I particularly wanted to start a family. Roo was totally indifferent, but we decided that if I was to fall pregnant, that would be fine, and if I didn't, that would be fine too.

Prior to having children, I was totally irresponsible and extravagant. I bought myself old sports cars when my overdraft permitted me to, and zoomed around like a big kid. I took great pride in my appearance – loved nice clothes, make-up and especially my long red nails!

I had tons of fun during my childhood with my brother and sister, to whom I am still very close. We all had a terrific time together, and I wanted *that* all over again through my own children. I could not imagine life without a family – I have always had, and love, company around me and I realized that once I had children I would never have to spend time alone. Being blessed with boundless energy and the knack of being able to do ten things at once in pure juggling mode, I didn't foresee any difficulty in adding a child to my busy agenda.

On reflection, I realize that looking through these rose-tinted glasses of mine, I only ever pictured having a toddler. I had totally overlooked the fact that there would be a baby first. Babies, to me, were like little aliens. I had never been exposed to one of those! But, decision made, we stopped using contraception and played a *very* long waiting game.

Out of the window went the theory, 'If it happens fine, and if it doesn't that's fine too.' It was not fine, and this situation made me feel desperate for a child. Every single month was filled with stress and strain. I became tearful each time my period reared its ugly head. If it was a day late I would use a home pregnancy test. The few minutes waiting for a positive result felt like hours. The disappointment each time felt like my world had come to an end.

And it nearly did one year on, when one evening I was doubled up in agony followed by a haemorrhage during the night. I had totally given up all hope of ever having children, but some hours later I was confronted with a positive pregnancy test. Through all the physical pain and fear, I almost jumped for joy. But this was short-lived. I miscarried one week later.

Back at home and a few months later hope welled up inside me. I put the idea of trying once again to Roo and we started all over again and again and again…

Making love was no longer spontaneous. The thermometer by the bed around the fourteenth day of my cycle told us when to 'have sex'. The science outweighed the passion. After the so-called fertile period, I refused sex on the grounds that it might cause an early miscarriage.

Finally, after two long and stressful years, I conceived.

But outweighing the excitement of being pregnant were the constant fears of miscarriage. I wouldn't hoover, iron, make love or do anything to risk losing this baby. My hormones were having a heyday. My emotions had gone crazy. I never seemed to stop crying. My family began to treat me like a celebrity, and admittedly I loved the attention I received. Having survived the first four months of this pregnancy, I actually began to enjoy it. During the last two months, though, I began to feel so, so tired, all of the time. The fear set in at this stage – I'd lie awake at night and realize the responsibility I was about to take on. I was filled with sudden panic – had we done the right thing? I woke up with this fear during the early hours of each morning and went to sleep each night filled with apprehension.

Georgina was born on 9 February 1990 following a very straightforward labour and birth. The midwife handed her to me immediately for a cuddle. I did not want to hold my baby. She didn't feel like 'mine' – she was not beautiful – she was wrinkled and ugly. I could not relate to her. I was taken to the ward crying as Roo left me for the night. I wanted to go home too, with Roo, without my baby – this little stranger.

Once on the ward, I was devastated by the total lack of support from the nurses. I had decided not to breastfeed and didn't want to, but received enormous pressure to do so, from all the staff. I didn't want to handle the baby, let alone put her to my breast. I watched my child sleeping and wondered how she could possibly belong to me. She was my responsibility for life now. I was petrified by this thought.

Roo arrived the following morning full of excitement about the arrival of his beautiful daughter. He couldn't wait to take us home. I was discharged not knowing how to bath my baby, change her bottom with confidence, or what to do when she cried. And when she cried, I cried, and never seemed to stop crying for a long time after that.

I was assigned a midwife until Georgina was ten days old, and a health visitor on the eleventh day. I was lucky – my husband had taken a week off work, and my mother came over each day during the second week to help me.

No one had told me to take things easy. On arriving home, the carry-cot containing a sleeping Georgina was put inside the cot, once our dog Yanni had had a good sniff around her, and out came the hoover and duster. I prepared mountains of food for the onslaught of visitors, and from that moment on, entertained a house full of family and friends for the next few days.

I began to feel that I had been sent home much too quickly. I was exhausted. I also realized that I still didn't know how to change a nappy, clean a belly-button, make up feeds, work the sterilizer, bath the baby or wash her hair. What should I do when she cried, vomited, wouldn't drink her milk? Yesterday I was a fat mum-to-be, today a mother. 'Take your child, go home, bring it up – good luck.' Should I lie her on her back, side, front, hang her from the ceiling? How should I cope when she screamed with colic pains? I could not sleep. I panicked when the baby woke up for a feed. I became emotional, with terrible mood swings. Roo didn't understand how I was feeling or why I felt as I did. I couldn't eat because of the constant lump in my throat. I felt as though I was continuously rocking a baby I did not even want to hold.

I couldn't stand the sound of her crying. It grated on my nerves. I didn't like her. She had made me feel like this. Roo couldn't handle her or me. He, too, was petrified of this tiny creature which had put such huge demands on our once perfect lives. I then began to resent every knock on my front door. I didn't want any more visitors. I didn't want them to see me not coping, or being unable to show this baby love. Was I not meant to have 'bonded' with my child and feel thoroughly enthralled by her?

It was so important for me to set a routine for Georgina so that a small amount of normality could be established in my chaotic home. But the visitors wanted to hold her, pass her around, feed her – totally mess up any routine I might have had. And then, she wanted to be held – she'd got used to it. And so I was left with the tetchy, crying child when my visitors went home. I hated them for leaving me. I resented them walking out of my home to a life of normality.

By now my mind had become totally confused. Conflicting feelings and thoughts made me feel as though I was on a constant roller-coaster ride. The home I had once loved and proudly admired I now detested. I didn't want to be there amongst all the baby gadgets and nappies. My weight plummeted and I was able to get back into my old clothes once again. But they never looked quite the same, covered in sick, dribble and bum cream. And I had to cut off those lovely long red nails. I couldn't risk scratching the baby. What had happened to me? My self-image was suffering beyond recognition.

I was depressed – truly depressed – and felt totally alone. If the whole world was in my front room, I would still have felt this terrible isolation.

The loneliness was even more evident at night. I could barely face those late feeds alone. Luckily, I had my loyal old dog Yanni to sit with me when Roo was fast asleep. She truly gave me the courage to carry on. I felt comforted by the fact that Yanni was with me and that my relationship with her could remain strong and unaffected. She was the only one in my life that never annoyed me.

After a few episodes of lonely night feeding, I just couldn't cope any more. On one particular night Georgina awoke at 2 a.m. crying. I dived under my duvet to block out the noise and realized ten minutes later that she had stopped. I was so relieved and went back to sleep. At 7 a.m., I had still not heard any stirring from the nursery. I thought the worst but at the same time was hopeful that I would never hear her again. That is something I will never be able to forgive myself for but feel that I must mention, for I am sure that many mothers have wished for the same in a moment of desperation.

Georgina did eventually wake up, I did feed her, but never again did she wake me up for a night feed. I had overcome a massive hurdle – no more lone feeds during the night.

A few weeks on and the novelty of 'the new baby' wore off … and so did the help and support. I was left alone with my baby – and she still cried and she still demanded.

The depression by this stage was nicely in place, only I hadn't recognized it. Coping with everyday life was a constant and on-going struggle. I began to resent my husband as he left for work each morning. What wouldn't I have given to walk out of that front door and close my life behind me. I was desperate to trade places with Roo – just for one day. I was so very low emotionally, and totally screwed up mentally. I started to bicker with Roo over the most trivial matters. This once fairy-tale marriage was appearing, to me, to crumble. I was scared. Roo, not being that interested in babies, didn't show any interest whatsoever in Georgina, wasn't particularly aware that she was even present unless she cried, and when she did, it put an enormous strain on our relationship. We were both uptight and each trying to protect the other from this alien little figure in our home. My conversation was solely 'the baby'. But what was there to say about her? She had slept, cried and poohed as usual. Where was this interesting exchange of daily news? Roo wouldn't talk about his day because mine had become so boring in comparison. He knew I resented his life.

One particular afternoon, my mother came over to find a screaming baby and a hysterical Cara. I was in a state of pure panic. What had I done with my life? I realized what it consisted of now. It felt like a prison sentence – the months stretching out ahead of me. The total lack of freedom. Why couldn't I bond with my baby? My mother was shocked by my complete honesty.

I no longer wanted this child. I didn't know what to do. Just shut her up and take her away. Mum offered to take Georgina away from me and to bring her up until I was feeling well enough to have her back. I couldn't understand how she could want her. She had brought up her own three children and was now prepared to take mine too.

The health visitor arrived during this traumatic episode and immediately recognized my devastation. She gently suggested that I visit my GP as soon as possible for some advice, and that perhaps I was suffering from post-natal depression – something I knew nothing about. Mum didn't take the baby home. I went to my GP. He told me, 'Well done for admitting how you feel. It is quite normal to feel as you do, and you will bond once the baby starts to respond.' I received *no* treatment.

Why hadn't my friends reacted in the same way? Perhaps they had – who knows what goes on behind closed doors? And so I had to accept that these feelings were normal, that I was doing everything I could for my child, and struggle on. Friends would contact me, excited about my new arrival, looking for news about the baby. I couldn't discuss her or my feelings. I should be happy and full of excitement. *I wasn't.*

Then I had to face the reality that my cupboards were bare. I'd force myself to go shopping, in total panic in case the baby started crying as I pushed the trolley around the supermarket. What would I do if she cried? What would other people think of me? I became petrified of leaving the security of my home.

I'd look at women without children and try to imagine what their life content was. I wanted to warn them never to have a baby. I was jealous of them.

I was living constantly on a knife edge and desperately needed the hour of peace and quiet when the baby was taking her nap. I then became obsessed about loud noises, for fear of her waking up too soon. It could be the doorbell, a few noisy kids outside, the telephone…I remember the telephone ringing and me screaming 'hello' so loudly into the receiver (out of pure anger and frustration) that it was that which inevitably woke the baby up, rather than the phone ringing in the first place! Or, on the rare occasion that she had actually fallen asleep on me, I would be scared to breathe, cough or sneeze – I so desperately needed that time to myself.

And this stage was so very, very boring. I didn't get to read a newspaper or concentrate on the radio or television. I felt totally out of touch with the real world. My depression was setting in deeper and deeper. My self-image had hit rock bottom – I was so desperate but did not know what to do. My mood swings were intolerable, and I hated and resented everyone who wasn't in my actual situation.

I never knew that I was suffering from post-natal depression – it was me, my fault, my problem. I had *no* professional support and no hope of getting better in the foreseeable future.

I then began to suffer from feelings of extreme guilt – the lack of bonding with my baby. I had bonded better with my dog and my rabbit – immediately. Why, so many months down the line, had I not bonded with my own flesh and blood? I wanted to take my child, dump her and run. I never wanted to harm her, but I wanted someone to take her away and love her like I felt I never had or could. I needed to feel young again. I was only 26 years old, yet felt old, frumpy and ugly. I had no inclination to dress up – what point was there when I would soon be covered in dribble or sick? This resulted in an even lower self-image. How could my husband still love or fancy me when I looked and felt as I did? I completely lost my sex drive. I was in desperate need of love but felt as though I no longer deserved it. I was constantly tired, moody and tearful.

I would find myself at the doctor's surgery with minor ailments at least twice a week as my physical health began to suffer too. I wanted to die and was hoping that something was seriously wrong with me. Each time I left the surgery I was actually disappointed that I would survive the latest cough or cold.

The tension in our household was like a balloon about to burst. I couldn't cope. I was scared. I wanted to go to work but my confidence would not allow me to. I was still fighting to hide this deep depression and trying so very hard to live up to false expectations. I was insecure, bored, and felt totally inadequate. If this was what having a baby was all about, then why did women have them? I hated the professionals for not warning me about these feelings. The ante-natal clinic had boosted motherhood up to such an extent. No one had told me the *truth*.

Once Georgina started to respond, perhaps with just a small smile, a gurgle or simply her following me with her eyes, I felt very rewarded to receive something back after months of blankness and so much effort on my part. It felt like a big 'thank you'. My life still revolved very much around feed and sleep times, but I did feel as though I was finally getting somewhere with her routine.

But one step forward and two steps back…I just couldn't seem to crack it! Although I felt a bit better about Georgina, I was most certainly not enjoying motherhood yet. Being able to recognize the baby's needs more did instil a little confidence in my actions, yet I was not confident or mentally strong enough to assert myself against conflicting advice, which you inevitably receive when you have your first child. I still felt like a bad mother, every move I made was wrong – the baby wasn't gaining enough, or perhaps was gaining too much, should be on solids, should not be on solids, needed more winding, had a bad tummy because I was not winding her correctly, should be dressed more warmly, should wear a hat in the middle of June, etc. etc. I truly did not know which way to turn or who to listen to. I could not listen to my own instincts because I did not believe in them.

Georgina was a hungry baby and I introduced solids quite early as she was not satisfied with just a bottle – however much I gave her. It most certainly didn't do her any harm, but I was plagued with fear after listening to all the adverse opinions offered to me.

My husband had still not bonded with the baby and offered me no emotional support. I was trying my hardest to be a good wife to him – I never wanted to let him down – and often pushed the baby aside to be just that. Then I felt guilty towards Georgina.

Everyone believed that I was coping really well. I had a wonderful way of hiding my true feelings. That made it more difficult because I just wanted to scream and cry in frustration. I remember talking to my mother one morning on the telephone and admitting that I just hadn't taken well to motherhood. I told her that I had absolutely hated the past few months and she told me never to say such things. She thought I was just having a bad day. Little did she or anyone else know that there were to be many more of those bad days to follow.

But, being an optimist, I believed that it really was still early days and that I would make it – somehow, sometime, we would all be OK in the end.

Georgina was now six months old and I was still trying to fathom why I did not feel better. Life was becoming easier, the baby was becoming easier and more enjoyable. She was a lovely little girl who had started to sit up, tried her hardest to crawl, responded very well, and was quite content to play with her toys or to watch a video. Why then was I still feeling so very low?

Being a reasonably logical sort of person, I sat myself down in a quiet moment and started to think about my situation. I began to compare the stimulation element of my 'old life' to my 'new life', and I think I came up with the answer. I was still utterly bored with the role of motherhood. Yes, I loved my baby now, but my husband still did not have any interest in her. This was a continual problem for me as I felt that the person I should be sharing my joy with was not remotely involved in our lives. This product of 'us' produced no response from him. I knew I had to just struggle on and go forward.

With extreme effort, I would take my baby to mother and baby groups and come back home totally unfulfilled by the nappy/shopping conversations which just didn't stimulate my ever active mind. I could not relate to these women who came to my home with their children. I hated the biscuit stains on the sofa, the beakers spilling Ribena on the floor, toys strewn across my living-room floor for all to trip over, not to mention the noise of babies crying as they grew tired during the afternoon. I would be exhausted when my visitors finally left, and hated the thought of preparing a meal after tidying up the mess and bathing the baby. I would look tired and feel distraught after this 'wonderful' entertaining afternoon, and had to face Roo when he arrived home, trying desperately to be the same old bright-eyed and cheerful female I had once been.

How on earth should my sex life have been at this stage? I'm afraid I just didn't have time to change into that sexy outfit after a nice relaxing bath, put candles on the table and prepare a gourmet dinner.

And then, Georgina was one year old. Did I still have post-natal depression or was I just not 'earth mother'? A question I cannot answer to this day. I had started to feel better. My depression was not constant. I still had bad days but began to have good days too. Georgina was toddling, much to my excitement; she had started to talk and had become very entertaining. She was a very happy child, returning my love in abundance and truly giving me a lot more pleasure. Roo's interest was sparked by her sudden toddling and talking, which I feel sure helped me to overcome my dark moods. We were finally sharing our child and enjoying her together. We had miraculously become a family after one whole year.

I decided at this stage to think about returning to work on a part-time basis. Although I loved Georgina, she and my friends alone were just not giving me enough of the mental stimulation which I desperately needed. Now was the time to look into good childminding facilities and to find some part-time work. A nice little project and a diversion from my normal train of thought. This was also the stage when we began to receive unwanted pressure, from family members, to add to the family.

At this moment I was trying to achieve something more from life now that I could mentally and physically face up to it – I did not want any more children. I could not face another year of deep depression – at least, not right now. But everyone had better ideas for us, and insisted that we give Georgina a little brother or sister. That was not very likely, anyway. Our sex life was still suffering – to me, sex meant babies and I did not want any more. If we used every method of contraception available, I was still paranoid that I would fall pregnant. I was just recovering from the worst period in my life, and Roo and I were coming through the worst patch in our marriage – I wanted to rebuild our relationship before I would ever consider having any more children.

By the time Georgina was three years old, life had become somewhat easier, and the memories of those nightmare months of depression began to dim. We never actually made the decision to have a second child, but for me, despite my experience of post-natal depression after having Georgina, there really was no question about it. I just knew that I had to have another one. I did not want another pregnancy, I did not want to go through the early stages of caring for a baby that I so detested, and I most certainly did not want to experience post-natal depression again. What I did want was a brother or sister for Georgina – desperately. How could I possibly deprive her of this? I knew that I would love my new baby (even if it did take me some time), and regardless of any depression. I also knew that I would forever regret not having a second child. I then spent a long time weighing up the pros and cons. The outcome: it would be easier to have a nightmare couple of years now than to regret not having had another child for the rest of my life. As for Roo, he definitely did not want more children. End of story. But I insisted, stated my case, and we stopped using contraception and played another long waiting game. I then experienced another early miscarriage.

Time was marching on, Georgina was getting older, and I became a little concerned about having quite such a large age gap. Here I was with a child approaching four years old, who was becoming quite an independent little madam and enjoying her nursery school, which in turn gave me some real space and time to myself. Did I really want to turn the clocks back now?

Then nature made the decision for me, I unexpectedly conceived, and once again gave everyone nine months of pure hell. Yes, I changed into the Incredible Hulk – with mood swings and emotional outbursts that could probably be entered in the *Guinness Book of Records*.

Roo came to terms with the fact that we were having another baby, but showed very little interest in this pregnancy. I continued to run about like a lunatic, now working part-time *and* entertaining Georgina. And once she became properly aware of the fact that I was having another baby, she became incredibly difficult – she started to wake me up at night at intervals, had terrible tantrums and got totally out of control. I began to feel the strain and found myself unable to cope with her outbursts. She drove me to tears frequently, which she seemed to regard as a real achievement on her part. I finally telephoned my health visitor about her difficult behaviour, and she visited our home and offered us some excellent and constructive advice. The book we were given to read and abide by was called *Toddler-Taming*. With all my strength and determination and the support of Georgina's 'fan club' of supportive family and friends who saw nothing wrong with her behaviour, we stuck vigilantly to the advice offered in this bible and were producing a much nicer child!

At 21 weeks pregnant, I developed terrible labour-type pains and lost a lot of blood. Feeling sure that I was going to lose this baby, I went into total shock. The bleeding and pain did eventually subside, but after this traumatic experience I was petrified for the duration of the pregnancy about losing the baby.

I had a much longer and more painful labour this time. After three days of mild labour and a nightmare of a midwife, Tasha was born at 7.30 p.m. on 18 October 1993. She was handed to me for her first cuddle – I felt elated with this child. I had not experienced this sudden rush of love the first time around. This baby was mine and I felt an inexplicable bond with her from that first moment. Nothing in my life will ever compare to the first time I held Tasha. My belly still does a somersault today when I think about it!

Georgina met her sister for the first time within an hour of Tasha being born. I will always remember her looking over that plastic cot with her eyes almost popping out of her head!

She was ecstatic and so was I.

Roo was suddenly very excited and quite smug, too due to the fact that we had another girl. He took Georgina home and I was taken to the ward with my baby girl. I received fantastic support in this hospital as Tasha was constantly being sick. I was discharged after three days feeling fit and confident – or so I thought.

This time things were going to be OK. With a few good nights of sleep behind me, and the experience of handling a new-born baby, I felt truly confident that I was going to win this time around. I was actually enjoying my baby and loved her dearly. But with the arrival of my milk, the 'baby blues' set in. I accepted my emotional state as just that, but when the baby blues didn't go away, I began to wonder if another bout of post-natal depression was about to rear its ugly head. I denied it. I coped. Tasha was still being sick after every feed, and this only ever seemed to worsen. I started to panic and was concerned that she would not thrive. The doctors and health visitors seemed very happy with her progress, though, and so I concentrated on trying to keep happy and healthy, while also struggling to make my older daughter feel included and entertained. As much as Georgina seemed to love the baby, she resented me. I was constantly holding Tasha as she cried for most of the time. She never kept her bottle down for very long at any given time, hence she needed feeding at least two-hourly. Because of her vomiting, I had to completely change her clothes (and often mine), cot sheets and bibs about six times a day.

Tasha would not settle for very long at any one time, which meant I had very little sleep and a completely disturbed household. Roo was petrified of dealing with this baby and hated it when she was sick on him. Therefore, he spent his spare time entertaining Georgina, which was a big help to me – in the beginning.

And so, a week or so down the line, things were not very peaceful, the whole family was becoming affected and little did I realize that World War 3 was about to erupt!

Roo returned to work, relieved to leave the chaos which his home now represented. I too wanted to leave the house and the responsibilities of motherhood behind me. However, I did love my children and my responsibility revolved around them. What could I do?

I continued to deny the obvious signs of depression which were creeping up on me, and fought hard to cope with my daily routine. I did not intend to go down that road again. Tasha was unfortunately becoming more ill. She began to projectile-vomit after every feed. It became a vicious circle – feed, throw up, feed, throw up. She would cry most of the time, and still did not sleep for very long at all. I found it more and more difficult to go out, because to do so entailed taking with me endless changes of clothes and the complete embarrassment of Tasha being sick all over someone else's home. Georgina was getting bored with the sudden postponement to her once busy little social life, and in turn I was feeling terribly guilty. I did not know which way to turn.

Eventually, my mother spent a day with me and commented on the fact that Tasha was looking positively ill. That evening after Tasha had vomited yet another bottle across the room, she convinced me to call the doctor, who immediately admitted her into the local hospital, saying that she was dehydrated. That is where she remained for a week, at five weeks old. The doctors suspected a condition called 'pyloric stenosis' which would mean a small operation on her stomach, but not before putting her through endless test feeds and close observation.

Going back slightly, I will add that Tasha would take large quantities of milk at each feed because she was constantly hungry. The hospital insisted that I had been overfeeding her and that we must cut her feeds down by at least half. This resulted in an extremely hungry baby, still throwing up the smaller bottle, and still crying constantly. I couldn't possibly sleep at the hospital with Tasha because Georgina was strongly objecting to my absence from home. So I was spending very long periods of time at the hospital, from early morning to late at night, just rocking Tasha to placate her, and then going home exhausted to bed, only to be woken up at regular intervals by a very distraught four-year-old. 'Nightmare' is the only word that springs to mind.

After five days in the hospital, the doctors decided that Tasha did not need this operation, but was suffering from a condition called 'reflux'. This simply meant my having to thicken her bottles with certain powders, to give the milk some weight, so that it would remain in her stomach. Tasha was discharged on the seventh day, and we brought her home feeling confident that her problem had been solved. Only it hadn't – in more ways than one.

She still vomited, still cried and never seemed to settle. Roo ignored her existence completely. He now strongly objected to her waking up through the night, which put an extreme strain on me. When I heard her stirring, my stomach somersaulted for I was afraid of his adverse reaction. Eventually, I insisted that he slept in another bedroom so that he got an undisturbed night's sleep. However, this did not help me. I could not hand Tasha over to Roo for any of the feeds, and found that the lack of sleep was only adding to my depression. I could not turn to him for comfort because I felt so angry towards him.

Roo did continue to help with Georgina wherever possible, but this, in turn, divided our family into two totally separate units. There was myself and Tasha, then there was Roo and Georgina. I felt resentful towards Georgina for having all of Roo's attention. In fact, I was devastated that he did not show any love towards Tasha or me. I felt totally starved of affection. I needed to be comforted, I felt so alone. All I had was my baby. Roo and Georgina were not mine any more – I had lost them along the way.

I now know that I would not have survived this turmoil without my dear friend Val, the domestic helper and childminder I employed, who helped me throughout as much as she possibly could (especially after the birth of Tasha). She became a dear friend – it was only with *her* support that I did manage to struggle through.

Because of Roo's lack of attention towards Tasha, I then began to overcompensate and gave her *all* my love. I gradually became very possessive of her and would only let Val or myself handle her. We were the only people I could trust. If the grandparents arrived, I would not even let them feed her. I was obsessed with her – she was my life now. Tasha, in turn, would now not go to anyone else at all. I had, without realizing what I was doing, made a lovely rod for my own back.

As time passed, I began to accuse everyone of not loving Tasha. I would verbally attack my family and in-laws, sometimes bringing them to tears. This obsessive thought stemmed from the fact that I truly believed that if her own father didn't love her, how could anyone else? More and more, I directed a lot of the blame towards Georgina. I'd say that she was the favourite child in the family, the 'blue-eyed girl' who could do no wrong. I believed it – I had to be right.

Being totally wrapped up in these distorted thinking patterns, I became more resentful, more depressed and more withdrawn daily.

Having recently been to the funeral of Roo's grandfather, I became obsessed with the thought that I had been possessed by some bad spirit while in the cemetery. I was not Cara any more. I never would be again. This feeling continued for many months and I blamed the evil spirit inside me for my thoughts and feelings. No one knew about this – it was my secret.

I gradually became so reliant upon Val that I would cry after she had gone home – she was my crutch to lean on and to get advice from, and of course, the only person I could hand over to when I could take no more. It was wonderful having her with me; her moral and practical support were the two things that saved me. I had a sense of freedom when she was with me, as she could and would willingly take over at any given moment. But outweighing the relief of her support while she was with me was the terror of her going home and leaving me. I began to dread the weekends without her, even if Roo was going to be at home. I never had his support or help – I might as well have been on my own with the baby.

I hated being alone for any time at all and would fill my home with my neighbours' children just to distract myself from my own situation.

As night-time approached, my stomach would churn and I would lie awake in the small hours planning the best possible escape routes. Suicide or running away. I would drift off into restless sleep, waking in a cold sweat. This continued for many months.

One day my health visitor came to visit me at home, as I had stopped showing up at the clinic. She immediately recognized that I was suffering from depression and sent me to the doctor. Val had pointed this out to me on numerous occasions but I had frantically denied it. My doctor was sympathetic and he gave me a course of anti-depressants. They didn't agree with me and had an adverse effect. But instead of going back to him, I then stupidly thought that I would try to cope without the pills.

By this stage, I had stopped going out completely. On the few occasions when I had made arrangements, I would get myself into a hysterical state before leaving the house, only to phone and cancel with lame excuses. I did lose some friends during this period, but realize now that they could never have been real friends to begin with. They had coped with their own children and could not understand why their bright and bubbly friend had turned so suddenly into an emotional wreck.

Out of sheer desperation, I decided to find an excellent doctor for Tasha who could sort out her feeding problem. I realized that if she began to improve, I would too. I did find one who suggested solid feeding early so that the milk would be weighed down in her stomach by the food. It also meant that Tasha didn't need quite as much milk as she was filling herself up with solids. This did help enormously, and slowly she started to settle for longer periods after each feed. However, feed times became very traumatic due to the fact that she screamed for her milk throughout the solid part of her feed.

With Tasha's feeding problem generally improving, and her sleep pattern becoming more routine, I could not understand why I had begun to feel even worse. Yet again, I blamed myself and withdrew deeper and deeper. Roo seemed oblivious to my state of mind and gave me no emotional support whatsoever. I didn't want him near me now, anyway. In my mind, he was to blame, but I never had the confidence to tell him that.

I was incapable of expressing how I was actually feeling. I knew that in time I would get through this, and everything would be OK again. But when?

I was feeling guilty, guilty and more guilty. I could not divide my time, attention or love fairly. Tasha needed me constantly – she was 'the baby', and a not very well one at that. Georgina needed me even more but I could not see that. She had her daddy – something neither Tasha nor I seemed to have. I resented her and was ridiculously jealous. She was the one that got screamed at. I blamed her for Roo not loving the baby. I blamed her for Roo not loving me. I blamed her for receiving all of the family's attention. I blamed her for everyone not loving Tasha. But this was not true. It was just the way my mind was working. Poor little Georgina had done nothing wrong at all. But it took me a long time to figure this out.

Georgina, being an incredibly bright four-year-old, was very aware that her mummy was 'not well'. She would look at me and say, 'Mummy, why are your eyes always watering?' That only made me cry more. It made me feel so guilty. I loved her desperately but didn't know how to show her that I did. I physically could not cuddle her any more. She was, at this time, very much a part of Roo, and I hated my husband. He, in my mind, was the cause of all my depression.

I went back to the doctor to tell him how depressed I was feeling and ended up telling him that Roo was totally unsupportive of me. He said that this was a large contributory factor to my depression and that if he could show some love to me and the baby, I would feel a whole lot better. But Roo couldn't. He still ignored Tasha and we spent many nights apart because she was still waking up for a night feed.

If Roo did sleep in our bed, we would end up arguing in the middle of the night about how 'naughty' Tasha was, while I was feeding her. I just couldn't cope with this situation. She obviously still needed the night feed and I was not going to deprive her of it because it annoyed Roo.

I was steadily becoming more and more dependent on Val and she was helping me for longer hours each day. She was very concerned about my state of mind, and although she never interfered, she would arrive very early and take as much responsibility from me as she could. It was a great help, but I felt guilty about that too. I was in a no-win situation. I did not want to be so dependent on her but could not live without her at this stage.

I continued to wake up in the early hours planning my way out of this dilemma. I wanted to die. I did not want this responsibility and could not see any other way of escaping. I would think about just packing my bags and leaving home for a while. I also needed to show Roo just how bad I was really feeling. I wanted him to *have* to take over my role for a while so that he would be more sympathetic if and when I did come back. I also considered dumping the children on my mother's doorstep and running away. It must have been my need to show the two closest people in my life that I was desperate now. But I did not leave home, and I did not dump my children.

I began to experience terrible aggressive rages which caused me to break things and violently kick doors. I would lock myself in a room and punch the walls and kick the cupboards and cry and cry and cry. I would wake up early in the morning crying and couldn't get back to sleep. The loneliness was so painful.

In desperation, I telephoned my mum and told her my secret – that I had been possessed by some evil spirit and that it was no longer me that dominated my thoughts. She was very worried about me and realized that I urgently needed help. She forced me to see the doctor again but now I came up against another problem. My regular doctor was away and the locum sat there and spoke to me. I told him that the anti-depressants had made me feel like a zombie and had had an adverse effect. I was even brave enough to tell him how ill I was feeling, that I was having aggressive outbursts and felt violently angry towards my husband. He told me that I needed these 'mind-benders' to put the chemicals in my brain right. I should get a book on pre-menstrual syndrome, and if I felt like hitting my husband, I should hit a punch-bag instead. He was so unsupportive, and made me feel a total freak.

He just about pushed me over the edge. I realized that once again I was going to have to find my own way to recovery.

I was becoming obsessively worried about my relationship with Georgina and knew that she needed a lot more of my undivided attention. It was imperative that I gave her some of my time – to play games with her and to show some interest in her little life. It was Val's teenage daughter who helped me out – she would just hold and rock Tasha if necessary, for a couple of hours every evening, which left me free to read, draw or just sit and talk with Georgina. This most certainly improved our relationship, and was the most important action I had taken so far. I had been beating myself up with guilt for too long, over how neglectful I was being towards my older daughter, when what she really needed, all along, was her mummy. Once we had established this regular couple of hours together each day, Georgina's behaviour settled down, we became much closer, and I slowly began to relax about that area of my life.

However, I still had the situation with Roo to tackle. We were not really communicating and I felt constantly angry towards him. Our marriage was going through hell and I really did hate him – and now I told him that. I was so very depressed and could not see any way out of this long, dark, miserable tunnel. Where on earth would it all end?

It was quite a long time before Tasha started to respond to me. But when she did, I was ecstatic. This poor little sickly child melted my heart when she smiled. I constantly battled with Roo to appreciate her little ways, but he still showed no response. Tasha began to settle down a bit now and slept for longer periods through the night. I was still deeply depressed and rarely went out of the house.

It was unfortunately the winter-time, which made everything feel more gloomy. My sister Lauren meanwhile had given birth to her first child, a baby boy called Bradley. Thankfully, he was healthy, happy and responding to everything very quickly. When we were together, I felt totally inadequate in comparison, especially as I knew that she was coping so well. Why wasn't I? When the two babies were together, no one would pick Tasha up because she would be sick on them but everyone would cuddle Bradley without hesitation. This hurt me terribly and only reinforced my protective feelings towards Tasha. Lauren could not understand why I was hating my role as a mother when she was enjoying it so very much. I could not begin to explain why. Her husband was enthralled with Bradley, helping at every moment and loving him constantly. I would watch him feeding his child, I was jealous when he kissed his son's head. What had I ever done wrong to make Roo act as he had towards Tasha? Surely she was just an extension of me and a product of our love. My mother loved Tasha dearly and would always hold her and love her. She too was very angry towards Roo but would never interfere. She did advise me to sit and talk to him, but I was not confident enough to do so.

I was scared that he would leave me while I was feeling so emotionally weak. I had absolutely no self-confidence and was petrified that he would take Georgina and go. I would have no argument at this point as I had not been showing Georgina much love for the past three months. And so I said nothing, and the time and situation plodded on.

Six months passed by and spring had sprung. The days became longer. The sun shone. I began to feel a little better. Better enough to say that I was no longer post-natally depressed but suffering from pre-menstrual syndrome for three weeks in the month. I was still not enjoying my life as it was, but remembered only too well that I had not enjoyed the early stages when Georgina was a baby. Of course, it was hard work – especially with two children. And therefore I made more of an effort to go out and about and start socializing again. Tasha was well established on solid food now and was not nearly as sick as she had been. She was sleeping right through the night and I was feeling much fitter. Val was still helping me with the children and suggested that I returned to work on a part-time basis. I jumped at the idea and went to work for two days a week in the City. It really did take my mind off my home life, but I frequently experienced panic attacks on the train.

I loved my 'days off' and didn't look forward to the days I would have to spend at home being a mummy. I wanted some more time to myself, away from responsibility, and once again I experienced the need to work full-time. But that was not possible. Even so, I was grateful when I could walk out of the front door for the day.

When Tasha was ten months old, my father had to go into hospital for a heart bypass. Although the operation was of a serious nature, it was apparently very routine, and within a week he should be home. I went to see him on the morning of his operation, and he never saw me again until three months later when he finally opened his eyes.

He had become seriously ill. I spent eight weeks, constantly at his bedside, in the intensive care unit. The family were told that he would not survive and therefore I could not be away from him.

Between them, my mother- and father-in-law and Val took complete charge of my children. I was never at home and became completely wrapped up in my time spent at Bart's Hospital. And I am ashamed to admit that although this was a devastating episode for me, it was a total relief to be away from my home environment for so much of the time. I felt like a visitor in my own home when I was there, and could give the kids a cuddle and a kiss and go off again.

I knew they were being well cared for, were desperately loved by their grandparents and Val, and were happily surviving without me. This was my way out. I would spend hour upon hour with my stepmother, who would listen to me, sympathize and advise. We would cry together for hours about Dad. All of my emotions surfaced at this stage. I would cry all day and then go home and cry all night. I did not know in the end why I was crying, but it was an outlet for all my pent-up emotion.

Roo seemed to understand how bad I was feeling about my father's illness, and gave me a lot of hope and encouragement. He spent as much time as possible at the hospital with me and insisted that my dad would survive. He would not accept things any other way. I willed my dad to live, to see his grandchildren, to be there for my stepmum, to be there for us. He could not leave us – I was too young to be without a dad.

And then it hit home – how could I have ever thought of leaving my children without a mother? Here I was crying for my dad to live and had only recently been contemplating my own death. I ran home and gave my children real love. I needed them and they needed me. And I needed help, which I would now make sure I received.

Dad did get better, very slowly, and I didn't need to spend as much time at the hospital. I found myself wanting to be at home with the children. My GP referred me to a psychiatrist, who I saw on a weekly basis. He put me on a long-term course of anti-depressants, listened to me for long periods, and put my whole life into perspective.

It was a long haul, but I could finally start to put the pieces of my life back together. The psychiatrist gave me back some confidence and helped me to assert myself again. He gave me the courage to sit down with Roo and tell him exactly how I was feeling. Being able to talk to this doctor brought all my anger and self-doubt to the surface.

With his help, I was finally able to take my life in hand and sort through my problems, one by one. Roo was the first step. Basically, I told him that I was going to leave home unless he showed some interest in the family – Tasha included. I could no longer accept the two units we had become and we all had to work hard at becoming a proper family again. Roo would have to actively involve himself with the baby and let me have some time with Georgina. He seemed not to have realized what had happened along the way, or just how serious I had been feeling about the situation. He was utterly shocked by my reaction and felt threatened by my statement.

He had genuinely not realized how ill I had been. I continued my treatment with the psychiatrist and Roo began to show a lot of interest in my progress. He encouraged me to see him and began to take a more active role in our home.

With Roo's support and love, I gradually recovered completely.

2

Rosemary

Rosemary married when she was 25 and left her job as a university lecturer in the UK to live with her husband in Switzerland. Her career was important to her but she could not find a decent job there because of different academic structures, and realized that all she could do was some paid research work.

Rosemary was using the coil as a form of contraception, and this gave her an extremely painful pelvic infection. She was told with total indifference by the first two doctors she saw that she was probably sterile as a result. The third doctor she saw put her into hospital for two weeks and did what he could to save at least one tube. He also strongly recommended that she try for children straightaway, as the younger she was, the better the chances were. Rosemary conceived quickly and was delighted. She had no problems during the pregnancy. The classes she attended with her husband on how to look after babies were confined to how to change nappies and how to give baths. The big day arrived, and Rosemary admits to having felt really nervous as she was about to undergo something totally strange to her. This was the first time that it had occurred to her that she and her husband were really different people. Until then, they had both been professionals with similar educations, but now she was having to do something quite essentially female.

The labour itself was painful, but the baby was a cute little girl who entered the world feet first. Rosemary recalls that the first time she held her in her arms was the most extraordinarily meaningful experience – probably one of the most dramatically wonderful moments of her life. She was glad that her husband was present, because he was the only familiar element during the whole process.

Things all went downhill from there. Despite that first wonderful moment, it still felt strange to Rosemary having this baby. She decided to breastfeed her, and found that this felt strange too. She left the hospital after one week with her new baby girl, a bout of cystitis and a high temperature.

Rosemary's husband had prepared a wonderful welcome home: he had cut out big letters saying 'Welcome home, from silver foil and put them in the hall. He was genuinely delighted with their arrival. 'As I had a temperature,' Rosemary says, 'I had to stay in bed and my mother arrived the following day when my husband returned to work. I already began to feel like a prisoner and I had a low-grade high temperature for three weeks. I was as weak as a kitten – like you feel with a really bad bout of 'flu. However, I had to get up every night once or twice to feed the baby who, unlike what the books said, became lively and wide awake during the night hours. Unfortunately, I am not a person who falls asleep easily and cannot nap, with the result that I seriously suffered with the lack of sleep. I remember dreading every night-time. My husband refused to do anything at night, pleading that he needed to be awake for work the next day.' Another problem that Rosemary had to face was the terrible night sweats (apparently the natural result of the change in hormonal activity).

'I felt and looked horrible, my self-respect tumbled to the ground and I felt like a prisoner without understanding what I had done to deserve this.

'How am I to describe those first years of motherhood? I fear that I could write a hundred pages and still not get across what it's really like. Psychologically, it took me two and a half years to get used to being a mother and for most of that period I was suffering from depression, although in the end just three months' counselling cured me of it.'

Ever since her daughter had been born, Rosemary had not felt contented. 'I felt frustrated, low, entrapped. I frequently cried and, quite apart from being woken up by the baby, I would regularly wake up after five hours of sleep and not get back to sleep.

'I especially felt a loss of my own identity. Before I married, I was in my own country surrounded by my friends and had good qualifications and an excellent job. I now found myself uprooted in an alien culture, with its sexless and jobless *hausfrauen*, with a language I could barely speak. I was perceived as just "another wife" by my husband's colleagues, and had a husband who felt frustrated with me because he did not understand what was wrong with me. Why was I not happy and radiating as mothers are supposed to be?! Our sex life was also almost nil – I did not feel like it – apparently normal with hormonal changes – but, in addition, I was unhappy and felt resentful towards my husband because his identity was untouched and he did not try to imagine himself in my shoes.'

Rosemary did not feel a strong bond with her baby. 'She was pretty, but my main feeling was one of being trapped with something strange that prevented me from carrying on life as normal: until then, if I felt like going out I simply put on my coat, then went out of the door. With a baby, going out becomes a whole operation – arranging the pram (in the first weeks I carried her in a pouch but later she became too heavy for comfort), and taking spare nappies, cleaning equipment, spare clothes etc. – this is because babies are frequently sick and when they go to the loo, the pooh frequently messes their clothes.'

Another problem Rosemary had to face was breastfeeding her daughter while out of the house. 'Despite all the encouragement to breastfeed, one was not allowed to do it in public; so one either becomes a prisoner, or, when out, one has to do it in some stinky restaurant loo. Just to add to my problems, both my babies [yes, she had another – read on!] had severe rashes whenever I tried to use disposable nappies of any make. I was forced to use cloth ones, which in Switzerland consist of three layers of gauze folded several times. Most of my life was spent washing and hanging out nappies to dry and the flat looked like a Chinese laundry. I am not a domestic person, and after a few months of this I was going crazy.' Thankfully, Rosemary had a cleaning woman who helped out once a week, cleaning the house and doing the ironing. However, she was desperate to get out of the house regularly without the baby. 'Just to add to my joys, my baby girl began to develop a terrible rash and stopped putting on weight at five months when I began mixed feeding.

'The doctors were hopeless and the specialist had the nerve to say that I was over-worried because she was my first child. Over-worried with a baby at eight months thin as a rake, weak and red all over? I tried stopping each new food one at a time so as to find out what caused it. The last thing I tried was cow's milk, and within three days the rash disappeared by itself and she began to put on weight again at last. I told the doctor that I had found the cause, but he told me it was not possible as babies with milk allergies vomit and mine did not. I am glad to say that I ignored him and she recovered. Many years later I was proved right – special tests showed that she is extremely allergic to cow's milk and will never be able to drink it, or eat cheese etc.'

Although Rosemary was still breastfeeding, she became pregnant with her second child, a son, when her daughter was just seven months old. 'According to the books, it is possible to be pregnant and breastfeed at the same time. I did so for six weeks, and during that period I felt constantly ill with exhaustion.

'The second pregnancy was also without major problems, but I began it exhausted and continued to feel that way throughout and he was heavier in the last months than my daughter was. I also developed thrush in the last month of this pregnancy, apparently fairly normal with the hormonal changes, but it was a problem that I did not manage to get rid of for about four years. That in turn gave me frequent and unbelievably painful bouts of cystitis which required antibiotics which made the thrush worse, and so on for years. The doctors were useless and the so-called specialist merely said that the way women are built makes these problems inevitable and there is nothing really one can do. In the end, I got rid of it by following the advice written by a woman in a book on the subject.'

When Rosemary's son was born, she had to contend with the joys of having a toddler around too. The toddler stage was Rosemary's worst age. 'Any semblance of being able to organize your life is at an end. You have to watch toddlers all the time to make sure that they don't kill themselves! They put everything into their mouths, cover themselves and everything else with dirt and food, do their best to break everything and reward you for all your hard work by regularly exercising their vocal chords in order to see whether they can scream louder than an opera singer! Of course, having no inhibitions, they succeed admirably and think nothing of having a tantrum of this sort in a café or shop.'

Inexplicably, Rosemary felt more of a bonding with her baby son than she did with her daughter. 'Perhaps it was because it just takes time to get used to being a mother. However, when he was born, I was totally exhausted, and although this baby did go back to sleep after he was fed during the night, *I* could not.

'Things were so desperate by then that I was beyond being exhausted. I was numb. I began using sleeping-tablets but became addicted to them and then consulted a GP on how to come off them. At the same time, I told him that I had been feeling low and dissatisfied with life ever since the children were born. He simply told me that I should not have had children and gave me some anti-depressant pills, which made me feel even worse and positively ill. I therefore stopped taking them.'

When Rosemary's son was three months old, she felt that she could stand life as it was no longer, and she just had to get away immediately. 'I arranged to go to Greece where my grandmother lived and rather surprised my husband that evening when I announced that I was leaving the next day for a week. If I could have left both children in Switzerland, I would have done so, but as I was still breastfeeding my son I had to take him with me. There is no doubt that the change of scene did me good, although unfortunately I developed another breast infection when there and did not sleep any better.'

About two months after this event, Rosemary's husband was told that he was to be transferred to London. 'I was really pleased about this and we moved when my son was eight months old. However, as I was going to my homeland, my husband expected me to undertake everything, including finding a house and all the other arrangements. In the normal way this would not have been so difficult, but, suffering from depression and exhaustion as I was, I did it badly and made mistakes. To this day he does not understand why. He found adjusting to a new country difficult, although unlike my situation in Switzerland, he had his secure job in London and was surrounded by his Swiss colleagues.

'However, he took his feelings of insecurity out on me by behaving like the lord and master of the house, and would complain that the housework and/or shopping had not been done correctly. I began to feel afraid of him, although there was nothing to be afraid of apart from his irritable moods and angry complaints. My feelings of depression got worse and I looked pale, drained and unattractive. My children were exhausting – both very lively, very loud and very, very messy. Life was a constant struggle against the mess which was like a monster with a life of its own. It is my misfortune that I am, by nature, a neat and tidy person and messiness irritates me. My husband, on the other hand, was perfectly capable of reading his newspaper, surrounded by chaos and totally shutting it out of his mind.

'It was actually possible to do the necessary work with a baby and toddler (both still with cloth nappies), if I worked without stopping from 7 a.m. to 11 p.m. every day. Ironically, the world calls this existence "not working", whereas a person who goes to an office to undertake tasks there for 35–40 hours a week is recognized as "working".'

Rosemary had made one friend in Switzerland, a Canadian woman, her age, who also had young children. 'Without her, I believe that I would not have survived those early years, for she gave me moral support that no one else did. My friend was working for a degree at the time and had also incurred everyone's disapproval. In Switzerland, you are firmly expected to be a *hausfrau* when you have children and all your qualifications are irrelevant. It was also her suggestion to have someone live in permanently in order to give me more freedom, which I duly did. My husband found me this "someone", but, as she was one of his relatives, she also disapproved of my wishing some time to myself on a regular basis. However, it did help considerably hiring the equivalent of a housewife, although, unlike a housewife, she gets paid and has evenings and weekends off.'

Rosemary can honestly admit that the early years of having children were the worst part of her life. 'I was now beginning to make some changes that were to improve things. I also looked through the phone book and found an organization that arranged counselling for women. Just being able to regularly speak to a sympathetic woman cured my depression in three months.'

3

Jane

Jane and Paul had only been going out together for a couple of months when Jane became pregnant with her first child, Daisy. Although the pregnancy was not planned, Jane had no doubt whatsoever about keeping the baby and was, in fact, thrilled.

The GP who gave Jane her positive pregnancy result wrongly assumed that she would not want to keep her baby because of the nursing course she was halfway through. She had a slight bleed when she was ten weeks pregnant and was convinced that she was going to miscarry. This same tactless GP then pointed out to Jane that many women miscarry in the early stages of pregnancy, which caused her a lot of anxiety.

Being halfway through her nursing course, Jane was living with Paul in her room in the nurses' home at the hospital. This they would no longer be able to do once they had a baby. They had problems with getting rehoused, but just three weeks before Daisy was born they managed to scrape together enough money to rent a flat five miles away. This meant losing contact with the women Jane had met during her pregnancy and, being preoccupied with moving, she did not have time to form any new friendships.

The house move caused further anxiety.

Daisy was born a few days early after an easy labour. But within just a few hours of her birth, Jane sank into a state of despair and was desperately unhappy during her three-night stay in the hospital. She returned home with Daisy, but had experienced problems with breastfeeding while in the hospital – these problems were quickly resolved, but all the same they caused Jane great concern. 'I had visions of Daisy wasting away.' She also had terrible fears of her baby dying and found it hard to take her eyes off her. Daisy was quite demanding and Jane was feeling tired, low and very aware of what a huge responsibility a baby was.

'Daisy was initially waking hourly throughout the night, and although we had plenty of visitors there was no one to give us any practical help at all. I can pinpoint the day that the depression really hit me. Daisy was a couple of weeks old and some family visited with their 16-month-old child. As she played about, I became obsessed with the thought that Daisy might die.' After Jane's family left,

Paul and Jane took Daisy for a walk. 'All I could do was cry, I wanted everything to end – I did not want to carry on living with this awful fear of what might happen.'

Jane couldn't enjoy Daisy for many months because of the thoughts of Daisy dying, which dominated her mind. She cannot remember her as a little baby because those early months passed in a complete blur. She was afraid to be left alone with Daisy, which Paul wrongly interpreted as a desire for company and practical help. In reality, Jane was afraid of what she might do to her baby.

Having encountered women with post-natal depression during her nurse training, Jane was aware of her symptoms, and did realize within just a few days of Daisy's birth that she herself was suffering from PND. Having worked with children for many years and having wanted a baby of her own, Jane had never entertained the possibility of becoming depressed, and she feels that no one apart from Paul seemed to recognize that she was seriously ill. She was extremely anxious about Daisy, but on the occasions she mentioned this to the midwife she was quite dismissive. Consequently, Jane felt unable to discuss her fears in any depth with her. Her health visitor, too, totally lacked perception and never recognized any of the early-warning signs that Jane was suffering from post-natal depression.

Jane's fears about Daisy were quite obsessive. She took her to be weighed every week – partly to gain confirmation that her baby was well and partly to escape the isolation she felt at home. Her greatest fear was that Daisy was going to suffer a cot death.

'When I mentioned it to one of the midwives, she gave me a leaflet which explained measures to prevent it. Even at this stage, my fears were so irrational that I thought if I looked at the leaflet, then touched Daisy, she would die. In order to prevent this happening, to "break the spell", I had to wash my hands. This "magical thinking" was to continue for many months about many different things.'

Jane's health visitor, although pleasant, never seemed to pick up on her anxieties. This caused her added confusion as she could not understand how she could be feeling so awful and no one else could see it.

'I was so frightened that Daisy was going to die that I decided that the less of a relationship I had with her, the less I would suffer if I lost her. I only had contact with her when I really had to. I had chosen to breastfeed her – it seemed to offer some protection against cot death – so I had to touch her to feed her, but otherwise I left Paul to do everything for her when he was at home. Everything I did for her, I did without making eye contact or talking to her. Often, I would watch her sleeping and sometimes, for an instant, I would imagine she had stopped breathing. This was the only time I felt relaxed – I actually felt relieved at the thought that all the months and years of worrying to come were over. On many occasions, I even considered suffocating her, in order not only to stop myself feeling so desperate but also because I felt that if I killed her, I could control how she died and prevent her from suffering.'

During these early stages, Jane had very little practical help or support and had no interest or enjoyment in anything. She felt completely numb and was in the most awful 'pain' and despair over Daisy. 'Apart from my main symptom of anxiety (which lasted for about two years), I was suffering from a compulsive disorder – "magical thinking and obsessiveness". When I saw or heard anything I believed could "contaminate" Daisy, I would have to wash before I could look at, or touch her. Even now, three years on, I still occasionally have to force myself to confront these thoughts. However, they no longer dominate my life and I don't now go out of my way to avoid newspapers, television and other formerly "threatening" issues or places.'

Another common symptom of PND that Jane suffered was a complete lack of interest in sex. She admits that her and Paul's sexual relationship hasn't yet returned to how it was prior to having children, but accepts that the realities of having a family – tiredness, lack of privacy and lack of opportunity – have a lot to do with this now.

The extent of Jane's depression wasn't picked up on for many months. 'Although I knew I wasn't well, I suppose I was able to cover up just how bad things were when other people were with me. Even Paul didn't realize the extent of my illness.' It wasn't until Daisy was six months old that Jane's GP referred her to Professor Brockington at the mother and baby unit of the Queen Elizabeth Psychiatric Hospital in Birmingham, and she was seen there for the first time when Daisy was eight months old. 'I attended an anxiety-management group and was prescribed "Imipramine". I had some reservations about medication, but by this stage I was prepared to try anything which would help me to recover. It took several weeks to feel much improvement, but, slowly, with support from Paul and the hospital, I began to feel more able to cope. During this time, the community psychiatric nurse [CPN] started to visit me at home.'

Jane had just started to improve slightly when she discovered that she was pregnant again with her second child, Jacob. Daisy was 14 months old and although the timing was not ideal, Jane did want the baby. 'For most of the pregnancy, my mood continued to improve and I continued to be seen by the hospital and the CPN. Towards the end of the pregnancy, I became quite anxious again.'

Jacob was born after a short and easy labour. Jane returned home within ten hours. 'Initially things went well and Daisy adored her baby brother.' However, Jane did relapse back into her depression. The CPN began visiting her more frequently and Jane started to attend the day service of the mother and baby unit again. She was prescribed a very high dose of Imipramine but found the first few months after Jacob was born very difficult.

'Things were not quite as awful as they were after I had Daisy, but there were times when I felt unable to cope, or to interact and bond with Jacob. Because I was already receiving medical help, I was more able to confront my fears. I remember feeling dreadful because when Jacob was distressed — for instance, if I was changing his nappy — I knew I should speak soothingly to him to try to comfort him, but I really just wanted to ignore him. With support, I was encouraged to handle him more, although this wasn't easy for me. When I began to have feelings and fears about Jacob similar to those I'd had about Daisy, the staff at the hospital helped me to deal with them.

'Another problem was that I hated not having adult company at home during the day and was always frightened of what I might do to the children when I was in the house on my own with them. I felt fear rather than resentment when Paul left for work — when he was with me it didn't stop the morbid thoughts I was having, but I felt reassured by his presence. After Paul left for work, my only concern was to survive until he returned.' Jane felt totally out of touch with the real world. 'I was isolated from former friends and colleagues, knew no one where we were living and, because of my obsessive-compulsive disorder, was totally unable to read or watch television. Paul and I had no social life as a couple whatsoever — I didn't enjoy being with the children but couldn't bear to leave them either.

'My self-image was non-existent. In the space of just a year, I had changed from being a happy, single woman to an anxious pregnant woman and then to a mother who could not even cope with looking after herself and a baby. I felt guilty about not being a good mother and cried to Paul about feeling useless and the fact that I couldn't even get being a mother right. I had difficulty in bonding with the children but I truly loved them. I just didn't want to become too attached to them as I felt so sure that they were going to die.'

Jane wanted freedom from the awful desperation she was feeling and felt that the only way to escape this situation would be if she or her children died.

4

Julie

Before having a baby, Julie and Michael had a fairly quiet social life but enjoyed eating out, holidays, cuddling up in front of a good film with a big bar of chocolate and a bottle of wine, and basically being able to do what they chose, when they wanted.

Julie worked as an employment officer in the Careers Service – a very fulfilling and satisfying job helping young people to get work. Julie and Michael had a very close relationship – they talked a lot, kissed and cuddled a lot and had a healthy sex life. Julie wanted a baby before Michael did, and she especially wanted a girl. She conceived quickly and easily – they were both elated.

Julie suffered from bad sickness during the pregnancy until about the fourth month, but continued to work right up until six weeks before the baby was due. She had always known that she would return to work full-time after her paid maternity leave, but began to feel quite depressed about this as the birth drew closer. A week before her confinement date, she was admitted to hospital with pre-eclampsia.

Julie was induced the following day, and as the labour was progressing so slowly, she went through numerous midwives as the shifts kept changing. Because of the pre-eclampsia and consequent high blood pressure, she was given an epidural (as this helps lower blood pressure) and, with hindsight, would recommend it highly. Many hours later, her much wanted baby Sarah was born.

Julie started to feel depressed while still in the hospital. She had decided to bottle-feed Sarah, and stuck to her decision, but did receive a lot of pressure from the nurses to breastfeed her. She was discharged from the hospital with Sarah after the fifth day.

On her arrival home she realized immediately that although it was a relief to leave the hospital, she had no one to call on for help. Julie had pictured life with a baby as very fulfilling. As she had experienced such a bad relationship with her own mother, she wanted the chance to 'make everything all right' with her own child. 'I knew that there would be hard times, but also knew that there would be lots of love and sharing as well. In reality, there *was* a lot of love, but I definitely was not prepared for the hard work a baby brings, the insecurity you feel as you're no longer centre-stage, the frustrations, anger, resentment, fear and responsibility.'

Michael, Julie's husband, returned to work and she was now realizing just how tiring and tying a new baby was. 'Just finding the time to take a bath needed strategic organizing.' Her mother-in-law, who Julie refers to as 'Mum', was very good, calling round each day to give her a break and of course to take over her granddaughter. 'I remember having a terrible cold, feeling totally drained of energy. Sarah was playing up (but of course she was too young to purposely create), and I couldn't cope. "Mum," I sobbed down the phone, "I don't feel well, Sarah's crying all the time, I don't know what she wants, help!" Devoted granny came straight round, packed me off to bed and trundled off with Sarah, leaving a saturated and inadequate mum behind.'

Julie did feel tired most of the time, and she feels as though all she was doing at this stage was feeding the baby, wiping up sick and changing her bum. 'The nights were even more tiring, as although we had a good rota system, Sarah was in our room and even if it was Michael's turn to shove the bottle in, I would be awake as well.' Julie feels that she made the mistake of trying to keep the house up to scratch as well as care for Sarah, and now realizes it was a stupid thing to do.

'I got obsessed about washing and hoovering. I was unable to ignore a pile of dried washing in a crumpled mound on the chair at 11 at night.' Michael thought she was totally mad, but that made her even more tired and irritable than normal. 'What I didn't realize until a couple of months later was that my madness was actually something quite normal for someone suffering from PND.'

Julie did feel quite close to Sarah during those first few weeks as she really was a good baby. Although she didn't resent Michael going to work, once he returned home she wanted a change of shifts. 'That poor baby was handed over quicker than a shot from a gun. I did love her but needed a breather, but why did I feel so guilty yet again? Michael was totally besotted with his new daughter and it helped that he took so well and so quickly to fatherhood. I loved Sarah so much that at times it hurt. Having not got on well with my own mother and now having no contact with her at all, I so wanted my relationship with my own daughter to be something special. This was another mistake, I now realize – trying to be "supermum" and ending up being a very frustrated and guilty mum for not achieving the goals I set myself.'

It also came as a great shock to Julie when she realized that outings were no longer spontaneous and that it would be two hours and large bagfuls of stuff later before she could even attempt an excursion. 'Decisions, decisions, one blanket or two, a hat or no hat, checking the time, calculating the next feed, enough nappies, bibs, changes of clothes, dummy, etc., etc. – all this to go to the local shops! It really felt like too much trouble to make the effort to get us both ready to go out, and this really didn't help to keep mummy sane.' Going out did them both good, but Julie was afraid to go out or, at other times, had no interest. Another sure sign of the depression starting – but she didn't know it.

'Freedom, what's that? Oh I remember, that half-hour spent in the bath! It would be easier if babies were in little pouches like kangaroos, as they are attached to you most of the time anyway. As for our social life – that revolved around our new addition most of the time, although we did have friends with children so we could now join the elite club we seemed barred from before.'

Julie found being at home with a baby was very different from going to work. She felt upset when she saw a 'temp' in her chair when she visited her workmates. 'Comments like "I wish I had all those months off on maternity leave with nothing to do" really got my back up. Did they honestly think that I sat on my backside all day? At least they got a full hour's dinner break and some mental stimulation.'

At this stage she had a very low self-image. 'I felt fat and frumpy while Sarah was just good enough to eat – life just isn't fair!'

Julie spent most of her time feeling guilty. 'Each time I yelled like a fog-horn as Sarah cried, I crumpled and cried later, feeling – oh so guilty. I wanted so much to be the perfect mum, so unlike my own, but I just couldn't make the grade. Yes, I'll admit it (it might make all you other mums feel better), there were times when I just wanted to cut and run.' Julie sometimes needed and wanted someone to tell her it would all be all right. 'I guess I went back to being a child myself at times, with tears and tantrums, sulks and sighs.' She spoke to a friend about her feelings of inadequacy, who she had thought coped much better than herself. 'Realizing she did the same things, it took the bag of guilt off my shoulders for a while.

'The fact that my mother-in-law coped brilliantly, never got angry when Sarah cried, could soothe her instantly and fed her better etc. was just about to cause further feelings of inadequacy, when a little chat with someone else explained that "grandma" wasn't quite so patient with her own two boys when she was younger!

'My mood swings weren't noticed by me at first, and if I was accused, I would defiantly deny it. I didn't realize that the reason I yelled quite so loudly when Sarah cried, why I couldn't be bothered to go out, argued with my husband, and literally didn't want to wake up ever again, was due to PND.'

During this period, Julie felt distant from her husband. He was very protective of Sarah, and Julie resented him a little, feeling for a short time that he loved the baby and not her. 'There was obviously a lot of tension between me and Michael when I was in a mood, and sex was totally off the menu – that didn't help either. My self-image was low – does Mr Blobby ring a bell?! Watching the "Baywatch" Barbie dolls didn't do much for my self-esteem either. I did take the time when I could find it to do my hair and make-up, as it did brighten me up – I wasn't having Sarah being pushed around by a frumpy mother.'

When Sarah was three months old, Julie had to return to work (Sarah was cared for by Julie's mother-in-law during this period). Her depression was ever present but not detected or admitted by her. It started to worsen after a few weeks back at work full-time. 'I couldn't cope with any stress at all, I spilled puddles of tears on to my desk during the day and growled grumpily at night at home. I was bullied into seeing my doctor by Michael, who was losing patience fast. This made me feel unloved, but in reality it meant he loved me a great deal.'

Julie's doctor put her on to some anti-depressant tablets, explaining that she was suffering from PND. 'I had read about PND once but really didn't understand just what it involved, but I was about to find out. The next week was tough all round. I was off work sick due to my "condition", but still cared for Sarah while Michael was at work. I didn't cope at all. Instead of relishing the thought of extra time with my little baby, I panicked. When Sarah cried it split my skull. I just wanted it to stop. I tried everything I could think of and she still kept crying.

'I just yelled and joined her. I couldn't control it. I went to bed that night and just sat and cried my heart out. A voice was telling me what a terrible mother and wife I was and how Sarah was young enough to forget me and that Michael would find someone else who was less trouble. Knowing Michael was downstairs, I started to take some tablets, crying as I chokingly swallowed them. I just wanted to be dead and all this pain I was feeling and causing everyone to feel, to stop. Whatever anyone believes or doesn't believe, someone decided that that night was not the time for my life to end. As if shocked awake by a nightmare, I realized what I was doing and knew that I couldn't die. I ran to the bathroom and tried to force the pills back out. (I don't know how bulimic people do it – be sick on demand, that is.) Pushing your fingers down your throat and keeping them there voluntarily is not an easy feat, and I definitely wouldn't be taking it up as a hobby! Once again I was a slobbering soggy heap. Michael came upstairs with what sounded like anger in his voice, but was in fact fear and concern. He demanded to know why. I just couldn't explain, I hurt deep inside – it was unbearable – and seeing tears rolling down his face hurt even more. I could see that he and Sarah wouldn't want to be without me.

'The doctor sped round, gave a sympathetic ear, upped my dosage of anti-depressants and gave them to Michael to dole out.' Julie now realizes that a suicide attempt or threat can be a cry for help. 'At the time I did mean to succeed, I didn't want to live like this any more, but maybe subconsciously it *was* just a cry for help. The one good thing to come out of this was that people realized that I wasn't *just fed up* – I really wasn't coping.' After this episode, Julie's mother-in-law decided to take Sarah from her during the day while she caught up on some sleep and did whatever she needed to do to make her feel better. Michael watched her like a hawk.

Julie began to 'chill out' a little more once the sickly side-effects of the prescribed pills wore off a bit. Michael did most of the caring for Sarah at night – 'He was bloody wonderful! I started to enjoy Sarah a little more, loving those first smiles and curious clutching fingers. I still feel cheated in some ways, though. I didn't enjoy Sarah as much as I feel I should have done, and I was taking medication all that first year and beyond. What I would have done without a partner like Michael to step in – well, that could have been a different story. I did a lot of screaming at Sarah but was lucky that most of my aggression was aimed at myself. Pre-period time was horrendous for me and my PND seemed to worsen.'

After a month off work, Julie decided she should go back, as grandma had volunteered to care for Sarah. 'I was a bit miffed that I had to go back full-time, but I also knew that even if funds had been abundant, I couldn't have stayed at home all the time.'

5

Pippa

Pippa and John had been married for 13 years. John wanted children. Pippa didn't. She wanted fun and felt no need for children. They had various interests as a couple, including the theatre, eating out, video and choccies, and were generally very comfortable and happy together. Pippa had given up her job in insurance one year previously as it was becoming very stressful, and took on a part-time job with the local council as a carer. She enjoyed helping old people, and her job involved helping to wash and dress them in the morning, getting them breakfast and shopping for them, etc. Falling pregnant was a great shock. John was delighted but also shocked.

Pippa was referred to the hospital early as she was forty years old. She was told to rest when she was five months pregnant because she had some pink discharge and had been doing a little more than normal. She was absolutely exhausted at this stage.

She had a long and hard labour, but gave birth to a perfect son, Callum. She was quite ill after the birth, and experienced terrible pain and fainting episodes while in the hospital. She discharged herself from the hospital and returned home after five days. 'I had always been told that life begins at 40 – I didn't realize that this is what they meant!'

As Pippa and John had both lost their parents and other family members lived so far away, it was just John and one neighbour who could offer any practical help on the return home. John took three weeks off work and he was perfectly confident in dealing with the baby. Pippa wasn't.

'He was little and wriggly and I didn't know what to do for the best – how to wind him properly or how to stop him crying. The first midwife who visited was OK, but the next one wasn't. We had an immediate clash of personalities. It was as if she had retired but had never told her employers. She was old and matronly with a very bad attitude. I was then sent another midwife – Claron. She was like a breath of fresh air. Nothing was too much trouble and she gave us good advice and always seemed to have time for us.

'I didn't totally breastfeed Callum but gave him one bottle during the day to enable me to rest. The only problem I had was with the positioning of the baby, but Claron gave me some good advice and helped sort that problem out. I generally found it hard to cope and it didn't help having no one around that I could turn to for help or advice. I wasn't prepared for that. I thought it would all come naturally to me – after all, I had read my "owner's manual" for advice! Callum fed every two hours and took one full hour to feed. I was exhausted. There was washing all over the house which took me three days or more to sort out. I could only tackle this chore when I had a bit of energy, which wasn't very often.

'I was not incredibly emotional, but felt quite numb at this stage. I had no self-image whatsoever and lived in a dressing-gown for the first few months. I just showered and washed my hair when I could. I never even looked in a mirror.'

Pippa did not have an immediate bond with Callum. 'It was seven or eight months on before I could say "I love you" and really mean it. They were just empty words before. I got on with my responsibility of looking after Callum, and John helped out whenever he could. He made sure that I ate, as I had lost all interest in food. I wouldn't eat unless it was physically shoved under my nose.'

When Pippa had been home for two days, she was still bleeding bright-red, and heavily. The midwife called the doctor out, who suggested she had a postpartum haemorrhage. 'I was treated with antibiotics and Ergometrine to contract my uterus and to dislodge the piece of afterbirth which was still retained. Although this did pass out, the Ergometrine affected the taste of my milk, making it bitter. Callum wanted my milk but wouldn't take it because of the taste. This was a very frustrating time. I felt angry and had had enough – I was numb, and so totally exhausted.'

Pippa could not at first tell the health visitor how bad she was feeling. 'She seemed very cold and unapproachable when we met. (She has since turned out to be an absolute star. I was even given her home telephone number. Our relationship improved so much and she offered me great support.)'

Pippa had no other support apart from a neighbour who would pop in to rock Callum while she walked the dogs. She was constantly exhausted. 'Although I was very irritable, I didn't see it as depression. My mood swings were awful, I really felt unable to cope.'

When Callum was about three weeks old, instead of him having his usual dirty nappy at every feed, he stopped going completely. 'After a couple of days of this, I was beginning to get very worried. I telephoned the doctor that night, and he came straight out to check him. He thought that perhaps Callum had a bowel blockage and I was told to take him to the QE2 Hospital. I was also told to pack a bag in case they kept him in. The paediatrician was waiting at Casualty for us – he looked him over and didn't think that there was anything wrong. (Apparently, breastfed babies sometimes do that. Why wasn't I warned about this?) Callum also had colic from the word go. We took him to see a cranial osteopath, and after about four or five visits he gradually got better. Between visits, we could see an improvement. Initially he would be better for a while, and then start to go downhill quite badly again. After the second visit he was better for longer and then went downhill, but not quite so badly this time. With each visit, the troughs improved. He was completely better after the fifth visit. This treatment really helped.'

Pippa always had feelings of guilt and doubt about Callum. 'Was he progressing as much as he should? Was he getting enough food? Was I stimulating him enough or was I overstimulating him? Was I overdoing this or underdoing that? It was horrendous.

'I started to feel as though I wanted to dump Callum and run. I even knew where I wanted to run to, which made it worse – knowing where I could go, it was more tempting. I needed the isolation of a place I had been to in Scotland. The need to do things that I hadn't done for years would unexpectedly creep into my head; I suddenly wanted to ride a horse again, had a yearning to do so. That feeling of freedom; the wind in my hair. Not to have someone hanging around my neck.

'I suffered terrible mood swings, emotional lows and irritability, and I would panic. At times, the panic would land in my throat – no words would come out. I really did not know what to do. I had no confidence in any of my actions. It was very difficult and I wasn't prepared for a baby. I felt and still feel resentful and angry about that too. I should have had some information before having Callum. But no one prepared me for this. I tried to live up to these false expectations all the time. I should be able to cope. I was feeling insecure, threatened and inadequate – why couldn't I cope? I'd see other mums when I was shopping and they seemed to be doing OK. I just knew that I wasn't coping well at all. Some days it was a case of taking things hour by hour, minute by minute. I'd think, if I can just get through this hour things will be OK, and then, if I can get through this hour, John will be coming home. If I can just manage for one more hour...full stop. It was one day at a time. When Callum cried, I didn't know what to do with him.'

There was one particular night that really frightened Pippa. Callum had been put to bed on a good feed. He had been feeding well for four months now and also had two bottles during the day. He had a breastfeed in the morning and a breastfeed last thing at night (when he would fall asleep on Pippa).

'It was 9 p.m. when I finally got downstairs to prepare the next day's bottles, and I heard Callum screaming through the baby monitor. I went upstairs. He was violently sick, which meant I had to change the quilt, all the bedding, our bed and his cot, him and me. He continued to scream and I just put him back in his cot as I didn't know what else to do. I turned him on his side and felt this urge to push him into the mattress to shut him up. I then realized that I didn't know what I was capable of any more. He finally went to sleep at about 11.30 p.m. and woke up at his normal time the following morning.

'I phoned my health visitor that day and was scared to tell her about what had happened in case my baby was taken away. She came round. I was in tears, depressed and totally miserable. She gave me a book to read to see if I could relate to any of it – well, I felt it had been written for me! John didn't understand what was happening to me. I just couldn't do anything – it was hard. Jenny (my health visitor) called the surgery. I saw my doctor that same day and was seen by a duty psychiatrist on the following evening at the hospital.

'I had reached a point where I couldn't sleep properly and kept on imagining Callum waking. If I did fall asleep and he moved, I'd wake up.

'As I decreased the breastfeeding, the PMT set in. It was awful – we used to call it "rat week". But this was something else. Now I couldn't even keep a civil tongue in my head. I felt so angry and would lose my temper completely at the drop of a pin – anything.'

Pippa could not keep control of herself and became worried about what she might be capable of now. 'It was frightening and I couldn't cope with Callum. Then, John had to go away for a weekend. I had pre-arranged for my friend, an ex-nanny of 23, to spend that weekend with me. Unfortunately she phoned and cancelled the day before. I was looking forward to her company and hoping to get some tips from her. That weekend alone with Callum was most definitely an endurance test. My nerves were completely shot by the time John came home. I was in tears and feeling drained, and although I had recently started some medication for the depression, it hadn't kicked in yet. At this stage it was making me feel worse – more confused – it almost exaggerated my symptoms. I didn't like it at all. The doctor at this stage was also exploring the PMT side of things. I was using Cyclogest pessaries ten days prior to my period, and taking vitamin B6.'

Pippa feels that this treatment helped with the PMT, which was a great relief. She also joined a PND support group. 'That really helped, just to know that someone else was suffering too, in the same way – I was not the only one who felt useless. We called ourselves the Yo-yo Club. One day you're up and the next day you're down.'

During these early stages, Pippa did start to regret having had a baby. 'I used to wonder what I had done. He was a surprise baby – not planned – and I felt like chucking him out of the window at times. He ruled my life completely, always knowing what he wanted and pointing to what he wanted. He was never content to sit. We even set up a play area for him which he never used. It was even difficult to change his nappy – I had to chase him around the room! My self-image was very low – I felt fat and over forty! I didn't like me any more. I didn't like who I was or what I had become – I wasn't even sure of who I was any more.'

As time went on, Pippa felt that life had become a bit easier, especially once Callum started to respond to her. 'I could relate to him more and his routine was becoming established. I didn't really have a day-time social scene but tried to see friends from time to time. I am still not confident, I am not stimulated, but I am not bored. I really don't know what would stimulate me any more. I still don't know what I am doing – it is a case of still working in the dark – I'm fumbling around. I often wonder if I will ever know what I am doing because every stage that Callum goes through is different and new. I have definitely bonded with him now. It is lovely when he lifts his arms up to be picked up. And that first squeeze back made a real difference.'

As for having more children? 'That is in the lap of the gods. Possibly, we will have one more.'

Pippa and John have since had a baby daughter – this time without PND.

6

Laura

Russell and Laura had been happily married for three years before deciding to have children. Russell had a good and secure job. Laura worked full-time for the Social Services. They enjoyed an active and good social life together. Laura is an outgoing, extrovert and confident character whose interests, prior to having a baby, included amateur dramatics and various kinds of voluntary work.

Laura conceived immediately, much to their delight, and deciding to leave no stone unturned, read every book on childcare and breastfeeding. Laura loved being pregnant and felt well during most of her pregnancy. She was admitted to hospital with toxaemia three weeks before her confinement date. Her heart rate and the baby's were monitored and Laura had her blood pressure checked hourly. She was induced twice during the next two days and underwent countless painful internal examinations.

She asked one of the nurses what the problem actually was, and quotes the very tactless reply: 'This is just to make sure that you and the baby don't die.'

Laura had to have an emergency Caesarean. Her daughter Hannah Gloria Green was born in perfect health. 'When I woke up from the general anaesthetic, the world "smelt" different. Because of the operation, I was not allowed to hold Hannah for the first day. When I did, she did not feel as though she belonged to me. I had an alarming urge to get up and run out.'

Laura suffered from the 'baby blues' in a big way while in hospital but, with hindsight, now realizes that there were many stress factors prior to conception which probably influenced her emotions directly after giving birth.

She arrived home from the hospital with Hannah. 'Russell was fantastic. He seemed to know what to do and when to do it. Even the nurses in the hospital commented on how easily fatherhood had come to him. Because I did not want to be there and felt so detached, it was a welcome relief.' Laura insists that if it hadn't been for his support and encouragement all the way, she wouldn't be where she is today.

'When I got home, people had already moved in, organizing my kitchen, my home and my life, which was alien to me because anyone who knows me agrees that if there is any organizing to be done, it is done by me. Having always been the pillar of strength to friends and family, it was difficult to envisage *my needing* any support from anyone else. I had not bargained for the fact that I would not feel maternal. I felt so guilty – the trigger of my descent down the ladder to post-natal illness. I thought that my family's perception of my maternal abilities was so high that even admitting to myself that I had a problem was too much to bear.

'Everything was being done to make sure that the baby was receiving the best care and attention. But where did I fit in? I found it hard to find a slot.' Laura remembers being very jealous of the time the baby demanded of her husband and other members of the family. 'I wanted all the attention instead – I had always had an incredible relationship with my father-in-law and to see him dote on Hannah so much made me envious. As selfish as it may sound, because of this I sometimes wished that she would sleep all day. When people used to come and visit they would completely bypass me and make a beeline for Hannah's pram, and although this was a totally unconscious gesture, I ended up feeling very unimportant. That is when I felt that something was not altogether right.'

After Laura had been home for two weeks, everybody, including the midwife, disappeared. 'It was like I'd had the decorators in – the dust sheets were off and so were they. I'd had little childcare experience and found myself wondering what to do. Why is it that by virtue of my sex, I am expected to know exactly what to do and how to cope? In fact, Russell was much better at it than I was.'

Laura started to worry because she did not have that 'bond' feeling that everyone had been talking about. 'Why was I different? It was at this point I decided that I, as a mother, was no good. Everybody I saw, in the street and at mother and baby groups, was coping so well and they appeared to be "natural" mothers. My own mother always maintained that having a baby should not disrupt your life too much, but that just didn't seem possible in my case. I later found out that my mother really did not disrupt her life – we just had to fit around it.'

Laura started feeling useless as a mother and wife. 'Getting up in the morning held new fears every day. My routine was relentless, and although I had no intention of going out at all during the day, I would be up before Hannah awoke, usually by 6 a.m. so that I could have a bath, make up, put the washing on, make the dinner and be ready for any eventuality. It was madness, as all I really wanted to do was to curl up and die.'

Laura started to write a diary of Hannah's development in her baby book, but occasionally wrote her inner feelings in there too. Two quotes from it: '9.4.93 – I'm depressed, people are telling me how great I look, but I feel like crap – how frustrating.' '18.5.93 – Can't cope, too much, I'm telling people how bad I'm feeling but no one's listening. I'm desperate, I need help.'

'Days would pass by when I would think how easy it would be to just walk out into the middle of the road and be wiped out. Or just go and never come back –

that way it would make life easier for everyone concerned and they could get on with the job of looking after Hannah properly. One day I even tried to prevent the health visitor from leaving my house by hanging on to her ankles for dear life. Odd behaviour, one might think, but not for someone who was suffering from severe post-natal depression. I just wanted someone to know how ill I felt.'

A few days after Laura's last entry in the baby book, she was admitted with Hannah into a private psychiatric hospital. 'It had taken two months for people to realize that something was drastically wrong and that something needed to be done.' She was diagnosed as having PND.

'I started to have intense therapy and was put on heavy medication, which spaced me out. There was no one there in the same position as myself and so I felt totally isolated. The staff were very helpful but none of them had any idea of what I was going through. The night nurses were prepared to feed Hannah, but they were very impatient with my lack of knowledge about childcare. A health visitor assigned to the hospital came to visit Hannah and I was so petrified of weaning her on to solids, I would pretend she was a month younger to put off the inevitable. Eventually the truth came out and I was encouraged to spoonfeed Hannah. Any change whatsoever, however small it might be, caused me great anxiety. Even weaning was a change.

'After I'd been psychologically prodded and analysed, I realized that this illness was not my fault and that I should not feel guilty that initially motherhood had not come easily.'

Laura stayed in the hospital for one month. 'Once discharged, I was set up in the "psychiatric community". A community psychiatric nurse visited me once a week to discuss the week's events, and my psychiatrist also visited me weekly. It took me quite a while to settle in at home and I still didn't feel as if I totally fitted in. Hannah and Russell looked *so* good together that I sometimes felt as if I was the intruder. Russell seemed to have a rapport with Hannah that I felt unable to even nearly match.'

After Laura had been at home for eight months, her psychiatrist decided that she had fully recovered. He took her off all the medication and discharged her from his care. 'I must admit, I did feel pretty good. I really believed I had seen the last of this terrible illness. This was not to be.

'Over the next month, the onset of puerperal psychosis went undetected and I started to decline, until one day I flipped and I was taken back into hospital kicking and screaming. The doctor told Russell that I had turned psychotic, although with hindsight I can see that this condition had been slowly developing. Russell was petrified. It appeared that I had not got to the root of my problem.'

Finally, after eight months, Laura was diagnosed as having 'puerperal psychosis'. Puerperal psychosis affects two to three thousand women each year. Normally, it is detected within the first two weeks after giving birth, but in this instance it was lying dormant until Laura's depression was triggered again months later. 'I was immediately sectioned for a minimum of six months and my husband had to give consent to me having ECT [electro-convulsive therapy]. I had to be sedated 24 hours a day. I was fed a cocktail of anti-psychotics and Lithium (a mood-stabilizer) to try to keep me under control.

'The furniture from my bedroom was removed because I was intent on hurting myself when not sedated. I became extremely violent towards myself and others around me. I remember one day I was convinced that the Devil was within me and I rushed out into the main reception, grabbed a knife from the left-over dinner trays and tried to puncture my stomach with it – thus releasing this beast within me. Russell was trying, along with the rest of the staff, to restrain me and I was quickly sedated. Sometimes, I did not even recognize my own husband – he felt destroyed by this.

'I cannot actually remember my first course of ECT but I remember having very odd thoughts which seemed to be normal while psychotic. I thought all the staff were going to kill me as I was possessed by the Devil.'

Laura remembers a lot of the unpleasant incidents in the hospital, and even with time, these memories have not faded. 'Russell came to see me one day, and because I was unsure of who he was, I would not let him near me. I would cower in the corner like a frightened dog if he tried to approach me. He later admitted to me that he was convinced that the Laura he knew and loved was never coming home, despite reassurances from the psychiatrist. Some days were a complete blur and others were literally a living hell. Eventually, the psychosis lifted, but I was still extremely depressed, still suicidal and very frail. I had withered to a seven-stone weakling.'

Laura was then transferred to Goodmayes Hospital where she received further ECT treatment, more drugs and intense therapy. 'The staff were all very pleasant at Goodmayes but I was still without my daughter. And even while depressed, I wanted her with me some of the time.' Because she had been admitted to an acute wing of a main psychiatric hospital, provision could not be made for Laura to spend days with Hannah while she was sectioned. 'Hannah would come to visit me, but it was like meeting with a stranger. The time spent away from her seemed like a lifetime and a lot can happen to a child in a short space of time.'

Laura and Russell had employed a live-in nanny while she was ill so that Hannah received some continuity of care. 'I had to get to know Hannah all over again. I was allowed home once a week to start off with, and then more frequently. I hated what the nanny stood for and the fact that she was living with *my family*, alone with *my husband* and *my daughter*. I feel sure that even a woman who was well would have felt threatened by this situation. On one of these weekend visits, I slit my wrists in front of the nanny. The nanny was of course very frightened and had to be persuaded by the family to stay. I suppose I was in so much mental pain, and

SURVIVING POST-NATAL DEPRESSION

at that time I felt that I had no other option. I really felt so "out of it" and that I would never fit in again.'

When finally discharged (after being an in-patient for a total of five months), Laura went home to rebuild her life. ECT had made her lose her bearings of where she lived, and she had to go around all the local streets to familiarize herself with them again. 'I felt so degraded, like an oddment in society. I felt so belittled that my nanny knew Hannah better than I did because I had spent so much time away from her. But, over the months that followed, our relationship grew stronger. By the time the nanny left, I had started to feel more like myself again.'

7

Gail

Gail started going out with the boy next door when she was 17 and married him at 24. They had an excellent relationship and a good social life including a mutual passion for the theatre. Gail was loud and outgoing, her husband placid and quiet. Gail conceived within the first year of their marriage, a very much wanted baby, and they were both ecstatic.

At eight weeks pregnant, Gail had a very worrying 'show' but the pregnancy continued without too many hiccups. She was extremely tired and felt very emotional and tearful during the last month.

She had a very difficult and painful labour resulting in an emergency Caesarean section after 36 hours. The midwives kept changing duty and Gail felt an extreme lack of continuity, not to mention a severe lack of information. She wasn't told what was happening, just had to watch the panic going on around her. Her husband was forever supportive, but this didn't relieve her from feeling petrified. Finally, her baby boy was put into her arms – she described this as 'pure ecstasy'. Just hours later, though, Gail was left alone and felt completely lost.

Her hospital stay was a nightmare, she had problems establishing breastfeeding and it seemed as though none of the staff had the patience to help her. Gail was utterly drained of energy and later found out that she was very anaemic and had been a borderline blood transfusion case. Nothing at all was explained to her. She had to work everything out for herself, and was sent home within a few days.

Gail and her baby left the hospital, Gail in tears. 'I had felt safe there and now I had no one to ask. It was all up to me now. I felt terrified.' Her mother was at home when they arrived back. 'I really had just wanted it to be the three of us. I know she had meant well, but it spoiled a special moment for us. The house was immaculate and looked like a florist's shop.'

Gail's husband went back to work earlier than she had thought he would, and suddenly things started to go rapidly downhill.

'I was alone with the baby and there was no one to ask what to do and I didn't know. Why was he crying, what did he want? I just didn't know. How did I bath him, what should I use? I hadn't a clue. Was he too hot, was he too cold? I didn't know. But surely I should? I was a mother. All mothers know instinctively what is needed, but I didn't.

'The panic worsened by the minute. I hated visitors. I felt as though they were looking and saying, "Look how awkward she is with that baby, she isn't a natural mother" – I hated doing anything for him when anybody was there. I'd go all hot and dizzy wishing they wouldn't watch and see how useless I was. I wouldn't answer the phone – I didn't want to talk to anyone. I couldn't watch the television or hold a conversation. I just couldn't concentrate, my mind was in a complete whirl. I couldn't read a book – the words wouldn't sink in and just danced about in my head.'

To add to Gail's problems, her doctor telephoned to say that she wasn't going to come out for the usual visit she makes when a patient has a baby. About six days later, another doctor phoned and said he would come out. 'He came, looked at me, then looked at the baby. He listened to his heart, then again, then again and again. My mind was racing – there was something badly wrong, I knew it. He pronounced a problem with his heart, shut his case and went. I was shocked and burst into tears, thinking my baby was going to die as I have a friend who had a baby who died of a heart problem.' This made it even harder for Gail to bond with her son – she didn't want to become too attached to her baby if there was a chance he could then die. His heart condition turned out after all the fuss to be just a murmur.

Gail remembers saying to her husband, 'I think that I am brain-damaged, something is wrong, I don't seem to be able to function and I just don't know why.' I was confused and very worried. I couldn't cook a meal – it was an impossible task. I'd put the cooker on the wrong number and burn it to a fraz or not turn it on and try to cook a meal. I'd cry and cry because I should have a meal ready for my husband when he came home but I just couldn't do it. I'd put the keys and the salt pot in the fridge and spend hours searching for them. I would cry because of these silly things where I'd normally laugh them off.

'I couldn't wash up, clear up or do the washing – they were just impossible tasks and I would cry. I couldn't even go in the garden to peg the washing out or get the baby ready in the pram. My mum had to come round and do it. When she did get him ready I'd walk him round to my old house [they had moved house recently] and stand outside howling my eyes out, wishing I was back there happy and in control – not this gibbering hideous mess I'd become. I was fat and ugly, a useless mother, and I hated myself. I hated being alone with the baby and would beg my husband to stay at home with me. He took as much holiday as he could, but still I needed him home. Every morning my mum would phone to see how I was and would come flying round as I dissolved into a sobbing heap. She'd come and take over and I would feel better. I remember lying over the cooker screaming that I hated my life and what I had become.

'I was in such a mess. My life was brilliant before and now I was living through hell. One day, I was lying in the bath and thinking, "If I just slipped under the water, it would be over and I would be free." It was my way out – an escape route. I didn't buy big packets of nappies as I wasn't going to be around to use them. I didn't buy any baby clothes as I wouldn't be around to dress my son. I was going away. I was either going to die or just run away.

'I really thought that I was going completely mad. My relationship with the baby began to falter too. I had to feed him, clean him and dress him. These were all chores to me and I just didn't want to do them. I was so pleased when I could hand him over to someone else and they did it for me. I didn't ever stop looking after him, but part of me really wanted nothing to do with him. When I left him for the first time with someone, I didn't feel guilt – just freedom. Then I felt guilty because I had felt that way. Where had the real me gone? And who was this uncaring monster that had taken her place? My husband loved the baby dearly and told him he loved him over and over again. I couldn't say it. I couldn't tell this baby I loved him. I hardly liked him. I felt awful but I just couldn't bring myself to say it.

'I was a terrible person and a dreadful mother. I was no good to either of them and I really should go.

'I cried and cried, knowing that I was finally falling apart. I was so desperate that I picked up the phone to call the Samaritans but I couldn't – they'd trace the call and take away my baby. My baby was so well behaved – he slept through the night and never cried. So why did I feel this way towards him?' After a while, Gail decided to bottle-feed her baby but realized that she didn't know how to use a sterilizer let alone make up a bottle. 'How could this person who could do accountancy for a multimillion-pound company not be able to make a bottle up?'

It took a while and a whole lot of courage for Gail to finally venture out of the house, and then only to be faced with further confusions. 'I hated the other mothers – all those people who could cope and look after a baby. Why couldn't I? I was always amazed when I went to the baby clinic that my baby had gained weight as I thought that I wasn't feeding him properly. I was sad and upset and my rotten health visitor had the cheek to say, "You have a beautiful baby boy – why can't you enjoy him?" If I could have, I would have. Didn't she realize the hell and frustration I was going through? Of course she wouldn't. She was a coper. Like my sister, mother to six and brilliant. Look at me, mother to one and useless.

'I remember my neighbour telling me ecstatically that she was pregnant. All I could feel was pure horror for her. She must be crazy to want a baby.'

Gail finally went to see her doctor with a friend, who helped explain that 'this in-control, bright, bubbly person' had turned, almost overnight, into a gibbering, confused wreck of a human being. 'The doctor hardly lifted her head, let alone spoke to me about my problem, as she wrote a prescription for anti-depressants.

This was just crazy. I used to be the most lively, outgoing person – why on earth should I be taking these drugs? I fought for days not to take them but eventually gave in. As a result, I became a zombie just wanting to sleep all the time – not wanting to get up, get dressed or anything.' Feeling even worse than before, Gail then went to a private therapist who she found to be 'far too deep' and absolutely no help. Again, this made her feel worse.

Finally, there was a glimmer of hope. 'I met a girl who had suffered from bad post-natal depression and who was now having another baby. So I wasn't the only person in the world to feel this bad. It was almost like looking in a mirror, hearing what she had gone through. She'd fought it and won, but I was so tired of fighting. She told me of a hormone specialist who had studied PND for fifteen years and used a rather controversial treatment of HRT [hormone replacement therapy] with quite a high success rate. I was willing to try anything, so after fighting with my doctor and private medical people, who all thought I needed to go to a psychiatrist, not a hormone doctor, they eventually relented and an appointment was booked.

'I was given a prescription for hormone patches [Estradol] and a promise that I would be cured in three months. I refused to use these initially on the grounds that all I had done was have a baby. I then plucked up the courage to get the patches and the pharmacist said, "Darling, if I were you, I'd get a counsellor, not these, they are for menopausal women." That was all I needed, and I ran out of the chemist's and decided not to bother. I'd fight on alone.'

Gail got steadily worse, making her husband come home from work in the middle of the day as she just couldn't cope. 'His patience finally ran out and he almost pinned me down to put a patch on me.' Very gradually things began to improve. 'I went to Tesco for the first time and did the shopping with my baby all on my own. Some people may laugh that my baby was three months old and I had not yet been out, but for me, this was a milestone and a massive turning-point.

'Things gradually began to get better and I remember going out in the garden one morning and thinking what a lovely day it was. The blackness was finally lifting. I began to go out on my own with my baby, go to the shops and visit people. I knew now I could cope if he cried or needed feeding. I finally knew what he wanted and didn't worry about people watching me. The old me was creeping back slowly. I hadn't gone – I'd just been hiding in the dark shadows. I began to enjoy my life again and most importantly of all, I began to enjoy my baby. We joined a mother and baby group, went swimming and out for walks together. I didn't mind mixing with the copers now as I was one of them. I didn't want to leave him with anyone any more and I wanted to do everything for him myself. I could finally say I truly loved him. I took great delight in flushing those rotten anti-depressant pills down the loo!'

Gail has since had another baby boy, but suffered a recurrence of post-natal depression when he was three and a half months old. Having tried anti-depressants the first time, she knew that for her this was not the correct treatment. Although Gail was living proof that hormone replacement therapy was the answer to her illness, and although she had stressed this fact, the doctor insisted that the only way to treat her was by prescribing Prozac (anti-depressants).

Gail had no choice, and in desperation had to take the tablets prescribed. Her symptoms worsened drastically – she was unable to cope and couldn't function without her mother there to look after her and the children. Eventually, after fighting with the doctor for a referral, she was able to see the hormone specialist. He once again prescribed a very high dose of Estradol (HRT patches).

Gail's symptoms of depression decreased almost immediately. Within just a few weeks, she had recovered completely.

8

Jenny

Jenny and her husband had a good relationship, and had always led a very active social life which only ever diminished for a couple of months after the birth of each of her first two children. She had worked as a social worker up until the time she had her first child and never had any desire to return to work after that.

Jenny found motherhood very fulfilling and satisfying and had never previously suffered from any form of post-natal depression. Her third pregnancy was not planned and was a big surprise – Jenny was 40 and her husband was just weeks away from turning 50. She found it difficult to tell anyone about this pregnancy as she felt ultrasensitive to what people said and thought – hence her anger towards an acquaintance who had said, 'What the hell does she think she's doing at her age?'

Jenny's husband really didn't want this baby. Although he was thoughtful and caring towards Jenny, he mentioned the possibility of a termination, but left the final decision to her. She decided to continue with the pregnancy but felt extremely tired, 'under par', and the seeds of depression were present throughout it. Because of her age, she had to have two amniocentesis tests, which were traumatic but showed the baby to be normal.

Her baby was born after a rather drawn-out labour, which left her feeling very tired. She was extremely upset to have a third girl, and often wonders if this was a main contributory factor to her depression.

Jenny arrived home within 24 hours of giving birth. Her husband, being in charge of a very large organization, didn't take any paternity leave. 'I do have help in the house and she is quite good, but she was a bit overwhelmed as I was usually an ace manager! My mother had offered to get me some help but I rejected this as I had managed so well before and felt her suggestion was rather interfering!'

Jenny felt extremely tired and emotional on her arrival home and started to panic when she realized she couldn't get to sleep. 'I coped on the surface with everyday life but, having done a project on bonding, was very, very aware of how important it was and became very anxious about it. I was also so aware of what a baby needed because of having had two, and did all that was necessary, but automatically rather than as an enthusiastic mother. I think knowing so much made me hard on myself, as I was very concerned about the psychological damage to my baby if I didn't respond lovingly all the time. I was feeling the responsibility of this baby hugely, and for the first time, didn't want it all to myself. My husband found this hard to acknowledge and didn't want to become involved as he didn't want his routine upset too much. He did, however, take the baby off on occasions to give me some rest, but I only felt guilty when I was not with her.'

Jenny feels that many of her friends found her difficult to take at this stage. 'This was not the very coping person they were so used to and although I never lost any friends, some certainly kept their distance, which I found most upsetting.' She found that after a couple of weeks some of the support did drop off, as people didn't know how to take her. 'The good friends stayed around. Some were truly magnificent and were there when I needed them, just to listen and support me – in fact for a whole year I had either a plant or some flowers on my kitchen table that different people had brought me.'

Jenny received unwanted interference from the midwife who visited her at home. 'She was elderly, not very confident, and made me lose my confidence. She suggested that I was not managing very well (a self-fulfilling prophecy if ever there was one), and she made me feel much worse. I am not usually like this with professionals, having worked with them a lot, but she seemed to undermine my confidence completely.'

Jenny began to feel trapped all over again at this stage, just when her second child was about to go to full-time school, which meant that she should be about to gain some freedom. She definitely felt depressed, very easily irritated, and very resentful of other mothers who now had some freedom. This caused her to feel very frustrated. 'I also suffered from a great feeling of depersonalization – being on the outside and looking in – being able to be with people but feeling outside, and in a way, observing them. We now kept our social life very low-key – in fact it changed completely. Even at my husband's surprise party which had been arranged by some friends, I felt as though I was on show – I hated it.'

There were many other symptoms of depression that Jenny suffered from. 'I still had the problems with sleeping, I wasn't hungry, was permanently tired and the enjoyment had gone out of my life. I had no sex drive, I didn't enjoy breast-feeding which I had loved before, and I could never seem to satisfy the baby. I had to supplement her feeds, which upset me, but I persevered with the breastfeeding too.

'If I slept well on the odd occasion, I didn't feel so depressed. If I slept badly, I used to feel awful and greatly concerned as to how I would manage my family. I tried extremely hard not to let the other two children suffer. However, my eldest was more than aware, when I cried, that all was not as it had been. She has since blamed the baby (as she was then) of causing me a lot of grief! This is all done in a bantering manner – true sibling love!

'I went to see my GP, who knew me quite well. He asked me if my behaviour and feelings were really "me". I had only gone to ask for something to help me sleep, which really was only part of the problem, but luckily, he picked up on my other anxieties. He put me on some anti-depressants and gave me some mild tranquillizers.'

Feeling very guilty about everything – the tablets she was taking, not being able to breastfeed satisfactorily, about how her mood was affecting the children, about how miserable it must have been for her husband to come home to a lifeless wife, about not feeling able to cope, about having negative thoughts about the baby, about being such a miserable friend – Jenny realized that things were not really getting any better.

'My doctor had recently suffered a heart attack and I had to see a locum, who was quite lovely, young, unorthodox and very supportive. He gave me a therapeutic dose of evening primrose, and when this didn't seem to work, he sent me to see a psychiatrist who was doing a project on PND. I saw her just once, and it was a bit like a catharsis, as from beginning to end I just cried and cried. But I did gain a bit more insight about myself from her questions.

'When the baby was about six months old, I took myself off the original anti-depressants and just used the Temazepam to help me sleep. It took a year, a whole lot of evening primrose tablets, a lot of support from my friends and husband, a baby that was very good, smiley and not so dependent, and giving up breastfeeding at 14 months which helped me to adapt to myself and the baby.'

Jenny would definitely not have any more children, although she feels that she has learnt so much about herself, and because of this doesn't think she would ever go through the same thing again.

9

Sarah

Before having children, Sarah thought she would be a good mum. She was very independent and intelligent, had a good lifestyle, and she and her husband Michael both had secure and interesting jobs with good salaries. They had nice meals out and generally had a good social life. Sarah had been made redundant in 1989 and had set up her own business working from home. She worked hard for the Women's Movement and had varied and interesting commitments prior to the birth of her baby Matthew. She was very much a career woman who was constantly 'climbing the ladder'.

Sarah insists that 'her body desperately wanted a baby'. She biologically needed a baby. It became a desperate need. Michael didn't want children. He did not want the responsibility.

Sarah loved being pregnant. She was blissfully 'fat'! She had no need to diet or worry about her weight or body shape now. It did not matter. She was comfortable and happy. She continued to work, but was getting used to the idea of being at home now. She kept up all her involvements in all of her interests and still chaired meetings up to one month before the baby arrived. She did find someone to take over her role as chairperson for the local Women's Movement branch, but with the intention of returning to that role as soon as possible. She had expected to 'get back on her bike and start pedalling' straightaway, but those ideas, unbeknown to her, were to go right against the wall. Sarah now says that she had no idea how tough things would be.

Sarah had excellent support from her husband Michael throughout the labour and the birth, but the midwives did let her down badly. Matthew was born at 8 p.m., but at that point the shift was changing. She quite rightly expected her midwife to see the birth through, but she didn't, and swapped shifts with another midwife just at the crucial moment when Matthew was emerging. The birth itself was exactly the kind she had not wanted – an epidural, induction, lying down on a bed and everyone shouting at her to push.

After the birth Sarah haemorrhaged, and she had been badly torn. After Matthew had been 'dumped' on her chest for a short while, she had to hand him to Michael while she was 'patched up'. She felt no desire at this point to take the baby. It was very important to her to look after herself in order to regain her strength so that she would be capable of looking after her son as soon as possible. Michael continued to nurse him for a long time while she recovered, and she feels that this is the reason why Matthew has always appeared to have a stronger desire to be with his father.

Sarah had very wisely chosen a private hospital because of the support and aftercare they offered. She had worked hard to build herself a good support network, had considered engaging just a private midwife, but chose the private hospital instead, which in turn offered her the support of a midwife counsellor.

She returned home after five days in hospital. As Matthew was born over the Christmas period, there was little support available. The community midwife did manage to visit, but each time it was someone different. There was no continuity, and Sarah felt very unsupported and lonely. She was having problems with breast-feeding and suffered from terrible breast pain. All the same, she was determined to continue. The pain was bad, Matthew was crying a lot, not settling after his breastfeeds, and he didn't seem keen on a bottle. The community midwife told Sarah that she didn't have enough milk and that her baby wasn't satisfied. She then tried to prove a point to her about her breastfeeding, by giving Matthew a bottle.

The midwife did manage to get him to take the bottle. Sarah sobbed and sobbed during that feed – she was devastated. After the bottle-feed, Matthew fell blissfully asleep. The midwife left feeling that she had at last proved her point, but just as she had departed, Matthew awoke, immediately proving to Sarah that the bottle had not solved her problem. He just continued to cry and woke up frequently. Sarah now hopes very much that he wasn't starving, but feels sure that she did not do any wrong by him.

The feeding problems and severe breast pains continued, and reduced Sarah to sweats and tears. 'I was still determined to breastfeed, but introduced an evening bottle which allowed me some "time out" while someone else fed Matthew. It did take some time before he really got to grips with a bottle, but after trying several different kinds, he continued to take this evening bottle. Ultimately, despite my upsetting experience with the midwife, I was glad that Matthew had now established this feed. It gave me an hour to myself, sometimes two, in the late evening when I could have a relaxing bath while Michael fed the baby and cuddled him while he slept. Sometimes my neighbour's nanny would take over this feed so that I could get my hair cut by a freelance hairdresser or have a massage.'

Sarah realized that she was now suffering from feelings of depression and after a period of general difficulty she decided to speak to the midwife counsellor. 'I eventually voiced all my negative feelings about various aspects, including how badly let down I had felt during the birth of Matthew. Having got all these feelings out in the open, I became quite ill with a fever. I cried a lot from that moment on. And it seems that once all my feelings had been released, my milk flowed freely and I never had to look back. My feeding problems were completely resolved.'

When Matthew was six months old, Sarah moved home to a new and much more isolated area, leaving everything familiar behind her.

'I was suffering from feelings of depression, it was the winter-time and I didn't drive.' This caused her further isolation, and coupled with the stress and strain of the house move, she began to feel as though she had absolutely no one to turn to. 'Matthew cried continuously and I couldn't concentrate on anything or even begin to think straight any more.'

Once settled in her new home, Sarah decided to find a childminder for Matthew so that she could resume some of her work interests. 'I found a child-minder for Matthew – he adored her and she adored him in return. I then found an excellent local nursery school where he could go for a couple of morning sessions each week. This gave me the space I so desperately needed, and Matthew was most definitely thriving there. I did not feel guilty as the nursery school was genuinely doing him a lot of good. Matthew has always had an extrovert character which needs a lot of stimulation. Feeling as I did, as well as not being able to drive, I could not provide the necessary entertainment for him myself.'

Once Matthew had turned one, Sarah began to face different problems. 'All the help and the support network I had initially built up no longer existed by now. I never met anyone like myself, who I could identify with – with my background or lifestyle. There were just no links with the people I met whatsoever. I then began to feel physically aggressive towards Matthew. I also had to contend with feeling exhausted for most of the time as he had never slept well, and the past year was catching up with me.'

At this point Sarah's childminder announced that she could no longer help with Matthew because of other commitments. 'This totally devastated me, not just for myself, but for Matthew too. I now felt as though there really was absolutely no one "there for me". I was constantly scratching for just a bit of help and never had any.'

Luckily, it was during this stage that the nursery school contacted Sarah and offered Matthew some more sessions. She immediately accepted them, which alleviated just some of the pressure upon her.

10

Veritee

Before she had children, Veritee was a senior youth worker in London, in a permanent relationship with Barry. Being qualified as a teacher and youth worker, she had always specialized in working with distressed young people and those with learning difficulties, as well as with young mothers and disabled children. She therefore had no illusions about the difficulties a baby could bring.

Her partner, Barry, worked at sea and had recently bought a cottage, closer to the port, in Cornwall. Although they could have continued their long-distance relationship, Veritee felt that the only way to establish a settled relationship would be to move to Cornwall. Being a very independent person with her own home, car and career, this was a very big step to take. She left London, and all she valued of her own, to marry Barry. As part of her new way of life, Veritee kept farm animals; soon Veritee and Barry's thoughts turned to having a child – happily, Veritee conceived six months later. Barry was supportive in the early months, taking time off from his job, as Veritee had a phobia about sickness and was continually *very* sick. She felt ill throughout the pregnancy and had to stop working until the fourth month, but then returned to work until the last month.

During the ante-natal visits Veritee felt as though she was being treated like a child. All her concerns about being an older mother (36 years old) were pushed away, and she did not receive any support on the subject of an amniocentesis test. No one registered her fears, and having worked with Down's and spina bifida children, she was aware of what could happen. She found the whole medical profession lacked any understanding whatsoever of her position.

The bad care Veritee received could perhaps have been due to the fact that Cornwall only had one independent private doctor and one NHS hospital with four obstetrics consultants (nicknamed 'the gang of four'). There was no choice in the matter but to attend this hospital, which was 20 miles away. Because of this 20-mile drive, she wanted her husband to be present when the amnio test was carried out in case of any problems. The hospital refused to arrange an appointment to suit her predicament and therefore the test was never carried out at all, causing her grave concern for the duration of the pregnancy.

Veritee stopped gaining weight at seven months pregnant, but despite her concern this was never investigated. They just told her that the baby was not very big.

She worried about post-natal depression after the birth because two of her relatives had suffered from this so severely that they became psychotic, and had to be hospitalized. She wrote this very clearly on her birth plan, but it was not acknowledged by anyone at all when she began to show symptoms of depression while still in the hospital.

Veritee was admitted to hospital with pre-eclampsia two weeks prior to her confinement date. She could hardly walk without feeling dizzy, and Barry was away at sea, which meant leaving all her farm animals on their own. She also had to get herself to the hospital, where she was put into a room alone and told to rest. If she tried to go and talk to the other mothers, she was sent back to bed. She felt lonely, totally isolated, had no visitors, no family to call on, and was worried stiff about the animals.

The doctor decided not to induce Veritee until after her confinement date, and managed to keep her blood pressure down until then. Barry returned from sea the day before her induction. Veritee was then in intense pain for two days but still wasn't getting any contractions. Not one of the hospital staff stayed with her, and she was told that she was 'just making a fuss'.

Apart from the pain, she spent most of her time in total disbelief. She had read the books, seen the films, and all the information she had received told her that she would never be left alone during her labour unless that was her own choice. She had by now become hysterical, but again was just told to 'shut up'. She cried for hours but got no sympathy. She was monitored only occasionally, and then, only very briefly. She was told that she was not having proper contractions but the baby was OK. She then suddenly started bleeding quite badly. The doctor came in and said, 'What is wrong with you now?' She had already called him in hours earlier and told him she felt that something was going very wrong.

Once he realized that she was bleeding, he tried to make excuses for her condition by saying that it was from the cervix and not from the uterus. The nurse rushed out to get a drip and had an argument with the doctor, who said it was not necessary. The nurse stuck to her opinion, though, and said she would rather the drip was in, just to be on the safe side, as she was worried about the bleeding. Veritee was then left for another few hours. By this time she was convinced something was very wrong indeed. She wasn't dilating, she was not getting any contractions, yet she was bleeding and in screaming agony.

Veritee knew that she does not normally react badly to pain as she had once worked for a week with appendicitis that then turned into peritonitis and gangrene. She was suffering more pain during this labour than she had ever done before. By now she could not move. The pain did not feel like healthy or productive pain, but still she kept being told that all was OK. Finally, she was sent to the medical labour room. She told the midwife to do something because she knew something was going awfully wrong. She was again told not to be silly.

Then, the shift rota changed. The newly assigned midwife attached a monitor to Veritee and there was sudden panic.

She was immediately given oxygen as the baby's heart stopped every time she breathed out. There was no anaesthetist available and they had to wake one up – they were not prepared for this at all. In the end, her Caesarean was done by the young doctor on duty as there was no surgeon available either. They kept saying that they had only three minutes to save the baby, everyone was panicking around her, and Veritee was lying there unable to move but trying to breathe deeply to give the baby oxygen.

Once the operation was over and her daughter had been delivered safely, the same young doctor who had pooh-poohed her complaints earlier stood in the doorway (obviously not wanting to be there) and said, 'You were right, we nearly lost you both and I'm sorry.' Unfortunately, there was no one in earshot and nothing could be proved. The baby weighed only four pounds at full term and was taken straight to the special care unit. Although Barry was sent out during the Caesarean, he held Caja as soon as she was born. He had an immediate link with her, but didn't seem to realize how serious her condition was. He left the hospital feeling quite happy, with a Polaroid photo of the baby.

Veritee, on the other hand, felt no links with her baby at all. Barry had taken the photograph home, and the baby was in the special care unit. Veritee had only a vague recollection of seeing her daughter just after the Caesarean. She was very ill herself and had drips and drains attached. After two days, she realized that she should have been taken to see Caja. No one had offered or encouraged this, but on her insistence they took her up in a wheelchair to visit her child.

For Veritee, nothing could be so far away from the idyllic picture of the new mother that the media like to present.

She was determined, despite being ill, that she would breastfeed her baby. After her first visit to the special care unit, she went up every two hours, day and night, which seriously deprived her of sleep. On one occasion, she overslept and missed a feed. Instead of being supportive, the nurse on the unit told her off, and fed Caja with a bottle. No one seemed to understand or care about how ill she herself was feeling.

Caja was kept in special care for about five days, but thankfully she was a resilient little baby, and the hospital were happy with her progress. But both Veritee and Caja then caught a hospital infection and were put into isolation. It was at this point that Veritee started hearing voices. She called a nurse but was told to lie down and rest. No one seemed to have time for her. She was very frightened and received no help. She also started to get migraines two days before going home, and these lasted on and off for six months.

She was sent home with her baby on the tenth day.

Once settled back at home, Veritee called the doctor out about her migraines. She was already displaying all the symptoms of PND but they were being ignored. Her biggest trauma was the total lack of support she was getting. She had just had a horrific experience and had felt frightened from the minute she arrived at the hospital when her labour had begun, right through to the worries about her baby in the special care unit. Barry was home for the first two weeks and did his best to help.

'He was genuinely over the moon about Caja. Things were reasonably OK while Barry was at home, although he did seem to cut himself off from me and Caja completely. He threw himself into DIY jobs and even took the roof off the kitchen on my second day home. This resulted in huge amounts of dust for the next six months.'

Veritee was in bed ill, her uterus still hadn't gone down, and she was taking heavy doses of antibiotics and Ergometrine. She was genuinely bedridden. 'I hardly ever saw Barry – he was on the roof or otherwise engaged with his DIY work. One day, he went to the pub and I became terrified. I counted the minutes until he came home. I was petrified and didn't want the baby anywhere near me.' This was an unexpected emotion and she realized that she had not bonded with Caja although she had been religiously breastfeeding her. 'The baby could have been anybody's. She didn't look like me and was unlike me in every possible way – she just wasn't mine and I couldn't relate to her as my baby. It was as if I had been given another animal to look after. She was my responsibility but I felt nothing for Caja.'

With hindsight, Veritee feels that perhaps this was because she had always wanted to see her own baby born and never did. She still finds it hard to believe where she came from. Veritee only ever had a small bump, never felt uncomfortable due to the baby's size, and was completely knocked out when she was born. When she woke up, the baby was there. She hadn't seen her born and feels as though she wasn't there. She never gave birth.

Barry had to return to sea. Veritee, in addition to the baby, had four goats, two ponies, one horse, twenty-five chickens, four cats and two dogs to look after. They had tried to get rid of some of the animals when Veritee got pregnant, but they were mostly rescue animals that no one wanted in the first place. The animals were great fun and seemed such a good idea before the pregnancy, and Veritee never expected to be ill.

'Emotionally, I felt like a zombie – as though I was not there. I felt dizzy and couldn't see properly, everything was "cotton-woolly" – I couldn't see Caja's face, couldn't make out her features – a very strange feeling that lasted for a good six months. Physically, I kept feeling faint and couldn't sleep. I was up every two hours feeding, but Caja was not thriving. I became so anxious and scared, and as soon as I did fall asleep I'd wake up after a brief doze when all my emotions came flooding back.'

During the day-time, Veritee felt that she had to do everything – washing, cleaning, ironing, etc. She even re-upholstered a sofa and broke in two ponies while Caja was asleep during the day! She also had to look after all the animals, keep in touch with work and attend the odd meeting. 'I had no help whatsoever except for one friend who came up to visit me with her two children about once a week when possible. This friend was also suffering from PND, and although she couldn't do any of the practical things, she helped me by just being there.

'When Caja was born, I hadn't lived here for long, and few people knew me very well. Because I had been working, I didn't keep regular hours at the shops and felt as though there was no one out there to care about me at all. Barry was at sea for long periods of time and my greatest fear was that if I died or passed out, no one would find me, and Caja would starve to death. I was scared stiff and taught Caja, at as young an age as possible, to crawl out of the cat door if necessary. I also began to get very worried about Caja's health. She seemed very frail compared to other babies. I became obsessed that she might die. I felt she was not well, but everybody told me I was being silly, including the heath visitor, and that the only problem at all was that I was not feeding her properly.

'It turned out that I was right and they were wrong. Caja had a heart problem which would account for her failure to thrive and her frailness, but this was not diagnosed until she was four and a half years old, despite constant visits to a pae-diatrician. I feel now that it was only my good care and my constant feeding her on demand that meant she remained as healthy as she was. I also had vague fears that I might accidentally (not deliberately at that stage) harm her by dropping her, or something. She really was very small and delicate and hard to care for.'

When Barry was home from sea they didn't sleep in the same room, as Caja was sleeping with Veritee in their bed. This continued for nearly two years because as she demanded feeding so often day and night, it was easier to have her in their bed. It was bad enough one of them not getting any sleep, and Barry couldn't feed Caja as she wouldn't take a bottle.

Barry could maintain the animals when he was at home, which was a great relief, and helped to look after Caja so that Veritee could tackle other tasks. 'We barely had any contact with each other when he was home. This did affect our relationship and things have never quite been the same since. We do not have time alone, and any time we do have is not the same time as we once shared together.'

Veritee had a health visitor appear once the midwife stopped coming. They didn't like each other. At first Veritee tried very hard to follow her advice and gain her approval. She felt very vulnerable and wanted to do things right – to have someone say that she was doing a good job. However, she soon realized that she could do nothing right. The health visitor seemed convinced that Caja's frailness and failure to thrive were due to Veritee's care, and gave her no positive feedback or support at all. Unfortunately, this health visitor was her only contact. 'Although she was in authority, she helped very little and refused to come out again after two visits.

'I then had to visit the clinic frequently because of Caja's being so small and having a weight problem. I didn't want to drive anywhere as I felt so ill. As well as the tiredness and all the other symptoms, I also had carpal tunnel syndrome [wrist problems] since the pregnancy, which made driving difficult. I still have it slightly, but I was made to go and see the health visitor. I had to go twice a week, and eventually once a week, adding a lot more strain to an already stressful situation.'

When Caja reached five months old, her weight gain stopped completely. Veritee had tried to wean her. At ten months old she weighed only ten pounds. She was tiny, delicate and fragile. At this stage, people started putting pressure on Veritee, as Caja had been doing fairly well at the beginning.

Veritee carried on feeding her, but Caja would just not accept solid food. She was then sent to see a paediatrician. Caja was mentally healthy, bright, lively and very demanding. Developmentally she was OK, but she was not gaining in weight or height. She saw the paediatrician monthly, and then at one appointment he said that Caja was ill – perhaps with a feeding difficulty or a growth problem – and that she had to go into the West Cornwall Hospital in Penzance immediately, without going home. The hospital was 40 miles from the one in which she was at that moment, and Veritee still felt ill and unable to drive.

At this paediatric interview they observed Veritee, and because she was unwell, even more than usual as she had a bug that day and felt particularly tearful and unable to cope, they doubted her ability as a mother. When Caja was sent to hospital, the purpose was to see her being fed. 'On our arrival, the hospital staff made it positively clear that they didn't want me to stay with her and I was very confused as I didn't understand why. Surely mothers were asked to stay with young babies, especially ill and underweight ones? I just couldn't leave Caja there alone so I took her home with me, and brought her back the next day. They thought I was so inadequate that I was just sticking her to my breast and not offering her solid food at all; that I was ignorant of childcare! Nothing could be so wrong.

'I had studied childcare at college and I had advised young mothers on childcare. I was offering Caja meals three times a day as well as breast milk, juice, etc. She refused to take enough and failed to thrive despite everything I did. The whole point of the hospital stay seemed to be to get her away from me. They were convinced that I was the reason she wouldn't eat. They thought that away from me she would start to eat and thrive.'

Caja stayed in hospital for seven days and caught a bug that caused her to vomit and lose even more weight. The hospital asked Veritee to express her milk so that they could test it, implying that something was wrong with it, and that was why Caja was vomiting. They were also investigating the possibility, unbeknown to Veritee, that she was not treating her child properly.

'I was treated as an ignorant woman in a patronizing manner. I insisted that I had been offering Caja solid food from three months onwards and that she just wouldn't take it. The hospital were acting as if I had never tried to feed her. But even their attempts at feeding Caja weren't working and I was extremely worried, thinking that my child was very ill – they never told me otherwise. No medical investigations were carried out at all – they just wanted to prove that I was an inadequate mother. At one point I talked to one of the staff, who I thought was a sympathetic nurse, about some of my fears about dropping Caja or not caring for her properly. My side of the conversation, but not hers, was later quoted in a case conference.'

The hospital continued to try to prove their point and offered Caja ice-cream, which is very obviously the nearest thing to milk. Of course, she took it. Barry was still at sea during all of this and Caja's weight was still dropping. Veritee, despite discouragement, went to visit Caja every day except for one, when she was too ill. The hospital actively discouraged her from visiting, yet at the case conference later, used the fact she had failed to come one day as evidence of her inadequacy. It was a 40-mile round trip, she was unwell, and would quite happily have stayed at the hospital had she been allowed to. By now, Caja was catching bugs and Veritee knew that this was wrong. She was healthy prior to going into hospital. They tried to put Caja on a drip and still wouldn't let Veritee feed her.

According to some teenage patients on the ward at the time, Caja kept everyone awake all night with constant screaming, as she was ill and suddenly denied the only liquid (and comfort) she would take – breast milk. 'I stayed at the hospital as much as possible after that because, if Caja would take the breast milk, I knew there would be no need for the drip. Nobody could get anything into Caja's mouth – she just wouldn't eat. It was not through my lack of trying.'

Unbeknown to Veritee, the authorities had planned a case conference for Caja. Veritee wanted to know why they wouldn't allow her to take Caja home, and went to see a hospital social worker whom she saw as her ally. She was a fel-low-professional, and at this stage Veritee trusted people in Social Services, and so poured out her heart to her. She was completely 'gob-smacked' when the social worker told her there was a case conference planned. Having worked with the Social Services, she couldn't believe that she had not been told that an investiga-tion was taking place. Veritee then went to a close friend who was a senior probation officer. The hospital were planning to keep Caja until the case conference, but this friend said that Veritee could stay with her, in order to make them release Caja.

'By now I was in a real state, feeling totally depressed. I didn't stay with my friend long as I still had the animals to care for. To my greatest surprise, despite all the concern shown and the fact that everyone was so terribly worried about my treatment of Caja, no one ever checked up on me, or visited me, from the day Caja was released back into my care until the case conference. By this time I was so distressed I would have welcomed a visit. If they were so worried about my care of Caja, why did they leave me alone with her in this state? If I was really so inadequate I could have done anything, stopped feeding her or neglected her completely. I was abandoned, waiting in fear for the case conference. I did try to delay it for a week until Barry would be home to support me, but they wouldn't hear of it. I desperately needed his support, but they wouldn't change the date. They did not seem to count Barry at all, and treated me as a single mother with a casual relationship.

'All this was happening to his daughter without him even having the option to be present! And what about me! All this time I was still working as a youth worker, I had Caja and all the animals to look after – I was busy too. The case conference date was not convenient to me. I was supposed to work that day and I could hardly tell my employers, Cornwall County Council, that I could not work that day as I had a case conference for my own child!'

Nevertheless, Veritee had to go alone to represent herself. She had no one at all. Caja was still ill but no one ever came to check on this child that they were so worried about.

Her probation officer friend tried to attend the case conference, but was told by her employers, whom she had to inform, that it would compromise her position as a probation officer. But she did go to see Veritee the night before, and helped her to prepare a speech. This speech was based on the fact that, because they couldn't find anything medically wrong with Caja, the authorities thought that Veritee was an inadequate mother and was starving her child.

Veritee had been back at work for three days a week since Caja was eight months old, and was sending her to a day nursery. Although the nursery could have testified, the Social Services wouldn't involve them. It was a fact that Veritee used to rush off and breastfeed Caja during her lunchtime break, and that the nursery's attempts to feed Caja in between had failed every time. The authorities were considering putting a care order on Caja before they heard Veritee's speech and even told her to leave while they completed the case conference.

Caja was not taken into care, but this whole situation caused great moral panic: no, this wasn't just some woman off the street – they were dealing with a fellow-professional. It was an awful situation for everybody.

At the case conference Veritee was allocated a social worker called Allwin, who claimed to have killed her own baby when it was six months old. Veritee first met Allwin at the case conference when she was sent to keep her company while the conference continued with Veritee excluded. This woman told her, while they were waiting, that she had never forgiven herself and always believed that her own baby had died because she didn't feed it properly.

How could they send her someone with this personal agenda? They obviously had already made up their minds that Veritee was also killing her baby through neglect.

'One of my enduring memories of that conference was a feeling of fighting for everything I valued. It was so important to convince them that I could care for Caja. I pulled myself together to do it. Barry and I had a good relationship, but would it have endured Caja going into care because I was considered a danger to my child, while he was at sea unable to do anything? Could I have ever pulled myself together enough to convince the authorities that I was safe for Caja if this had happened? I do not think so. I now believe I would have sunk into real mental illness. Everything I valued would have been destroyed. I would have lost my family, my husband and of course my job. I could not have continued to be a youth worker with my own child under a care order, or on the at-risk register, because of fears that I would neglect or harm her. My job was very important to my self-esteem, and in many ways it was holding me together as something I still felt I had some skills in.'

Another thing that Veritee remembers, at the end of the conference when it had officially finished, was that she burst into tears and told the chairperson of her fear that Caja was ill and might die. The woman, Maria de Main, replied that they were frightened she might die too, thus increasing Veritee's fears. It was only later that she realized that Maria meant that she was worried that Veritee's actions would kill her! 'The only good thing to come from the conference was that they changed my health visitor to a woman called Danielle Moon, who was wonderful. She gave me good help and advice. I wish I had known her from the start.'

A family aide was then sent in to check up on Veritee, but she could find nothing wrong. She knew that Veritee wasn't neglecting her child. She was sent in at feed times to watch Caja being fed, and could see that Veritee was doing everything possible. 'It felt as though everyone was convinced that I was the problem. This all got too much to bear, and three months after the case conference, at my request, they finally withdrew from my home – they had absolutely no proof.

'They offered me free childcare and other things, but I just felt that their involvement was damaging, as it was only on the basis that I was somehow bad for my child. I knew I was now very depressed, but I was never offered help for this, which I would have welcomed. I was never offered treatment despite the severity of my depression. At one point I went to the doctor and insisted he refer me to a psychiatrist. This doctor did not treat me. He seemed to think that as my baby was now over a year old, I did not need help. He gave me his contact number and told me to come back if I ever had post-natal depression again – if I had another baby. Why couldn't I get the help I so badly needed?'

This whole experience with the hospital and Social Services had totally disrupted Veritee's life.

Once the case conference was behind her and the Social Services withdrew, Veritee had to spend nights alone with Caja and she became scared. She was by now physically ill through her depression and extremely angry with the changes in her life that the baby had made. She felt she would have got over this if the Social Services had just left her alone and she had instead received proper treatment for the depression. She began to resent Caja for this experience, but managed to repress her anger towards her. She then started to feel as though something must be wrong with her if all this could have happened. The experience with the Social Services had completely shattered her.

'My self-image hit the floor. My job was now under threat as my boss had been made aware of the situation. I started to resent Caja and felt that it was all her fault. I also began to feel that if so many professional people thought I was an inadequate mother, there must be some truth to this. It felt as though my whole life had been shattered through having a baby. I had nowhere to go. I even reached a stage where I wanted to kill Caja – I wanted Caja out, anywhere but near me. I had even planned it all in my mind. I had been made to feel like a criminal and began to think that I must be the worst thing for my baby. After all, there can't be smoke without fire. What had I done to bring a child into the world who was not thriving? I started to feel as though the world wasn't a good place, and if this had all happened in such a short space of time, what would happen during the rest of Caja's life? I didn't want her to suffer and needed to take her away from it.

'There is a lot of deserted countryside near to where I live, with lakes, bogs, rivers and woods, and I'd walked through them with Caja on various occasions, seriously thinking about throwing her in there. No one would ever find out.' Veritee knew that nothing could have stopped her if she had decided to take action. She had the means to do it. Because of these thoughts, in the middle of the night when Barry was away she threw all of her sharp knives down the mineshaft at the back of her garden. She could no longer trust herself alone.

Throughout this period Veritee rightly insists that it was the mother who needed the support – not the baby. If she had received the much needed support from the beginning, instead of the constant criticism and blame, it would have helped *her* recovery. But no, they were only interested in the child, even though by protecting and helping Veritee they would in turn have been protecting and helping Caja.

Veritee had constantly received the exact opposite of support, and because of this she was now having these terrifying thoughts against her child. Even if they had taken Caja into care, she knows that she could have still killed her if that was what she really wanted to do. 'You can do anything in five seconds if you want to. By working with the mother, it would have benefited the child. They were not protecting Caja whatsoever. They were fuelling a resentment over which I had no control.'

Realizing she desperately needed some help, Veritee paid for private counselling weekly, which at first was very expensive. She had two different counsellors, one who was very kind and supportive at first, and another who was more challenging – who designed her own treatment. The counselling Veritee chose had no links with government agencies – they were independent and she knew that she could say what she wanted and needed to. The private counsellor felt that Veritee wouldn't harm her child and said that she would report her if she believed that she would. She felt it was only a fear.

'Once I was completely over the feeling that I might kill Caja, I attended a child and family centre which was free of charge and is run by the health authority, not the Social Services. I am deeply grateful to my therapist Christine Small, who has been very sensible about the things I have told her. I could not risk the Social Services getting on to me again.'

The centre definitely helped her. Although Veritee started going there with her own problems, she has now developed a professional relationship with them through her own work.

'Having a telephone counsellor through the Association of Post-Natal Illness really helped. I could tell the counsellor my worst fears and thoughts knowing that I would never meet her. She had gone through the same thing and her child was now seven years old. She listened to me when I was really angry. Thank you, Rebecca, for listening to my baggage even when I was making no sense – even to myself.'

Since all of this happened, Veritee has been told that things have changed – but she doesn't believe it. She is involved with the Social Services through her work – she hates recommending people to the system.

She was later asked by the senior social worker why she did not just play along with the system for those six awful months. She advised Veritee that this would have been a lot easier. However, for Veritee, it was totally against her principles. They had entered her life uninvited, and she would not tolerate that. Had they offered her the right kind of help, the help that she needed, she would have gone along with it, but because she is a clever woman and fought it, what she experienced was nothing less than a trauma. A less articulate or less educated woman would perhaps have had an easier time in some ways, because she might have gone along with it all not knowing that she had a choice. The authorities just made it harder for Veritee – they were worse than useless when she was feeling physically ill and this threw her over the edge, which in turn made her want to kill *herself* over a further two years, not Caja.

When Veritee was just beginning to recover, a young woman from the village where she lived did kill herself. Veritee believes that she, too, was suffering from PND. This suicide had a profound effect on her. 'Karen's baby was a year younger than mine. I was not close to her, she was much younger than me, but my husband was very friendly with her husband. I always thought that Karen was suffering from depression. I could sense she was suffering like me, and felt distressed that because of my own illness I could not help her. She was a lot more withdrawn than me and talked to few people. However, she did know I knew how she was feeling. Once I found her in a distressed state pushing her baby in a pram round the village. I spontaneously said, "You are pushing her round because you are scared you will harm her." She broke down and talked a little about it. All I could do was sympathize – I could do no more as I was so ill myself.

'Her baby was only three years old when she killed herself. By this time her relationship had broken up and she was living alone. She did have the Social Services' involvement, but I presume for the same reason that they were involved with me. In fact, she killed herself while her daughter was in the Social Services' care, to give her a break. I have no idea if she had treatment for her depression. This affected me for many reasons. I felt guilty because I had known her suffering but had done nothing. I was still feeling suicidal and it proved to me that it could be done. One thing that had stopped me doing it was the thought of leaving Caja without a mother, but Karen's daughter was taken on by her father, and he managed very well.

'The child was with a stable parent instead of a depressed one, who after a few years married again. It confirmed my fears that Caja might be better off without a depressed mother. But most of all it depressed me that the system had so let this young woman down. With all the help she was supposed to be getting, she still died a lonely and distressing death at her own hand. What could be worse?

'Why does society fail to cope with this very common illness, PND?

'I coped with my feelings by looking after Karen's child over the next year when I could, even though I was still ill myself. Her father used one of our out-buildings for a workshop, and I felt that by having their child, and giving her father a break so he could do some work, I was doing something for Karen that I was unable to do when she was alive.'

Veritee feels that another major factor in her depression was that she was finding it hard to be responsible for someone. But this gets better all the time, as her child gets older. 'As Caja has become older, I know that she can survive without me. This is always niggling with me – always will be with me – this responsibility thing.'

Summary

Having looked closely at the ten personal accounts in Chapters 1 to 10, I have tried to identify some common factors which may have contributed to the onset of post-natal depression in each individual. I asked all the women included in the book to relate a little bit about their life prior to having children, and their personal experience of the pregnancy and birth. I feel this to be an important issue, as one of the points of this book is to show that although we all had different personal circumstances and backgrounds, and each took different routes through life, we have all finished up at some point in our lives with the same experience – post-natal illness.

Common factors

1. *All 10 of us were confident, outgoing characters.*

   All 10 of us were independent.

   8 of the 10 were career-orientated.

These three factors alone could contribute to the mothers becoming depressed because of the drastic and sudden change in their lifestyle after giving birth. They have to become responsible for another human being and they may feel a sense of dependency (financial or emotional) on their partner which they didn't experience beforehand. Looking after the needs of a young baby in comparison to a fulfilling job, for most career-orientated women, can result in a severe lack of mental stimulation. If they feel unstimulated or bored with their role, it is natural to feel depressed about the lack of excitement in their lives.

2. *4 of the 10 moved home before having a child or when the baby was very young.*

Moving home is a major stress factor. Adapting to new surroundings and feeling unfamiliar in those surroundings only add to the insecurities already being experienced by a new mother.

3. *3 of the 10 pregnancies were unplanned. 1 was unexpected.*

An unplanned or unexpected pregnancy can be a great shock – a wonderful surprise for some families, admittedly, but for others a huge disruption to their lives. It can be very traumatic to adapt to the idea of having a new-born baby, and may entail some difficult and emotional early decisions – especially if any doubt about keeping the pregnancy is expressed by either partner.

4.   *5 of the 10 women suffered seeds of depression during the pregnancy.*

These seeds of depression need to be closely observed during ante-natal care. If a depression is evident ante-natally, the chances of getting post-natal depression are much higher. If the factors relating to the depression are dealt with and treated during the pregnancy, it can save the whole family from the destruction caused by the mother's mental illness, which is likely to worsen post-natally. (See 'Ante-natal detection' by Ann Herreboudt, page 125.)

5.   *4 of the 10 had a 'show' or threatened miscarriage.*

Having experienced two miscarriages myself, I know that this can instil a terrible fear of losing the baby during the earlier stages of a pregnancy. It takes the enjoyment out of being pregnant and results in extreme anxiety and uncertainty. In an extreme case, the fear transforms into paranoia, resulting in thoughts of giving birth to an abnormal or stillborn child.

6.   *2 of the 10 had very poor ante-natal care.*

8 of the 10 had a bad labour or birth experience.

4 of the 10 did not have the continuity of a midwife during the birth itself.

The joy of being pregnant can be very short-lived if the ante-natal team are unsupportive. It is very important to feel secure, assured and confident during the pregnancy. If a mother is not confident with her ante-natal care, her doubts, insecurities and resentment towards the ante-natal team may well surface after giving birth, resulting in a depression later on. The same applies to women who have had a bad labour or birth experience.

7.   *5 of the 10 experienced an immediate difficulty in bonding with the baby.*

This factor comes under the heading of 'Disorders of the mother–infant relationship – delay' (Professor Brockington, page 122).

8.   *3 of the 10 had poor hospital support after giving birth.*

4 of the 10 were discharged from hospital very early.

Once back on the ward, it is vital to receive good support from the nurses – help with feeding, bathing and general handling of the baby. The mother is often discharged very quickly if the birth has gone smoothly – before the milk has arrived and the 'baby blues' set in.

The given uncertainties and insecurities, and dealing with possible 'baby blues', in a home environment can contribute largely to the onset of PND. If support from the hospital nurses has been non-existent, the mother can often feel nervous and unconfident in dealing with her newborn baby, not knowing why it is crying or why, perhaps even more importantly, she herself is crying.

9. *4 of the 10 were ill immediately after giving birth.*

Most women expect to feel tired and a little emotional immediately after childbirth. It may prove difficult to get back on your feet even under normal circumstances, but if you are then physically ill, it can take a lot longer. After any physical illness one often feels under par for a while. To have a new-born baby to care for in addition to feeling unwell oneself is extremely difficult. This factor, once again, can lead to feelings of depression – especially if there is little practical help available.

10. *4 of the 10 had ill babies.*

As with a threatened miscarriage, the consequences of having an ill child or even thinking that your child may be ill can take the enjoyment out of motherhood immediately. Some mothers become so fearful of losing their baby that they refuse to bond with it. As you will have seen in Chapter 7, Gail suffered from this fear when she was told that her baby had a problem with his heart. In a less extreme case, apart from the anxiety for the baby's well-being, the mother may have the added strain of dealing with a baby who perhaps cries persistently and/or demands much more care and attention generally.

In the following summary, I have focused on the common symptoms and stress factors expressed throughout the personal accounts. They most certainly suggest the onset of post-natal depression, although perhaps they could easily be confused by the individual concerned, with general tiredness, prolonged 'baby blues' or the difficulty in adjusting to a new routine. All the symptoms mentioned below should be questioned immediately and not accepted as normal. If they are discussed with a health professional and treated correctly at this early stage, the chances of a prolonged depression will be greatly reduced.

I have broken the summary down into three sections: the common symptoms, some facts which might have contributed to the depression or made the symptoms more severe or prolonged, and finally the effectiveness of various treatments which led to recovery.

Common symptoms

1. 5 of the 10 lacked prior experience in caring for a baby.
2. 4 of the 7 who breastfed experienced feeding problems.

3. All 10 experienced difficulties in bonding with the baby once home (5 of us had developed this lack of bonding immediately after delivery).

4. 4 of the 10 expressed a hatred of the baby crying.

5. 5 of the 10 felt an urge to harm the baby.

6. 6 of the 10 felt afraid of being left alone with the baby.

7. All 10 developed a 'loss of identity' and a low self-image.

8. 7 of the 10 had difficulty sleeping.

9. All 10 described a feeling of isolation and loneliness.

10. 8 of the 10 lost their libido.

11. 7 of the 10 felt resentment towards their partner.

12. 4 of the 10 developed problems in their relationship with their partner.

13. 8 of the 10 described a feeling of general, undirected anger.

14. 9 of the 10 had general negative thoughts and feelings.

15. 6 of the 10 began to set themselves false or unnecessary goals.

16. All 10 experienced feelings of general anxiety or panic.

17. 6 of the 10 became physically ill.

18. 7 of the 10 wanted to die or felt suicidal.

19. All 10 experienced extreme feelings of guilt.

Facts

1. 6 of the 10 lacked practical help. 2 of those 6 also lacked their partner's support.

2. A further 2 of the 10 lacked their partner's support (totalling 4).

3. 5 of the 10 returned to work.

4. 6 of the 10 women in this book suffered from a bad childhood experience.

5. 1 of the 10 suffered post-natal depression for less than one year.

6. 4 of the 10 suffered PND for 1–2 years.

7. 5 of the 10 suffered PND for 2–3 years.

8. 3 of the 10 later suffered from severe pre-menstrual syndrome.

Treatment and recovery

1. 6 of the 10 were treated with anti-depressants (they were effective for 4 of those 6).

2. 3 of the 10 were treated with hormone therapy. (This led to a complete recovery for Gail, but only helped with the symptoms of PMS for Pippa and Julie.)

3. 4 of the 10 were prescribed tranquillizers, which helped reduce the anxiety attacks but didn't cure the depression.

4. 8 of the 10 had counselling or were seen by a psychiatrist (effective for all 8).

5. 5 of the 10 feel that support groups were effective in their recovery.

6. 8 of the 10 feel that the support given to them by their partner or friends greatly contributed to their recovery.

7. 5 of the 10 began to feel better once they resumed their career or work interests.

8. Although all 10 expressed a desire for some time and space to themselves, 6 actually felt less depressed once they had developed that freedom on a regular basis.

Conclusion

Despite going through the awful experience of post-natal depression, 5 of the 10 women went on to have another baby. Perhaps they, as I did, thought that post-natal depression wouldn't occur a second time around, especially with the experience of motherhood now behind us. Unfortunately, 4 of these 5 did have a recurrence, but recognized the symptoms and requested help from their doctors much earlier, which resulted in a quicker recovery.

The Other Half

The first and last parts of this chapter have been written by Dr Malcolm George, who has spent many years researching PND from the husband's point of view via the Men's Studies Research Group, Department of Physiology, St Bartholomew's and Royal London Hospital Medical School. The rest of the chapter consists of interviews with some of the male partners of the main contributors to this book (those willing to speak), together with comments from the women about how they felt about their partners at this time.

Men behaving sadly – not badly

Post-natal depression, by virtue of its very name, has an inexorable association with pregnancy and the experience of women after the birth of a baby. It is perhaps the form of depression that is most completely seen as 'feminized' because of this association, and anyone could be forgiven for believing there is little need to discuss a woman's male partner in relation to it – other than perhaps to echo the heartfelt feelings of women who have experienced PND and who feel they received precious little practical or emotional support from their male partners.

It is to the author's credit that, having felt much the same way within her own experience, she has since been able to see that a discussion of male partners and PND may have plenty to benefit both women *and* men. This view can be supported by evidence from the academic and medical research of PND, and depression generally. Thus it is a pleasure to be able to have the chance to offer some perspectives, which will hopefully be of help to both partners when a baby is born.

Depression, in general, and post natal depression, in particular, are seen as feminized problems. It is quite possible to argue from a professional viewpoint that this is a mistaken view, but it has to be recognized as a lay reality. Many assume men are generally less likely to suffer from depression, and few would intuitively accept that some men become post-natally depressed! In fact, recent research has identified that a significant proportion of the male partners of women with post-natal depression also become post-natally depressed themselves, and that some men become depressed following the birth of a baby even when their partner is not depressed.

Perhaps the most important point to make and discuss in this chapter is the fact that coping in a relationship where one partner is depressed is extremely difficult for the other partner. The personal accounts given later attest to this fact amply. It does not matter whether it is a man trying to cope with his depressed female partner, or a woman trying to cope with her depressed male partner.

In a relationship in which depression strikes, the other partner cannot be considered 'neutral'. Indeed, there are negative effects from the depressed partner to the other, although these tend to differ slightly depending on whether it is the man or the woman who is depressed. The mood of the non-depressed partner is lower and the couple's interactions marked by negativity. Thus, for instance, couples in which one partner is depressed tend to report less relationship satisfaction and more interpartner conflict than couples who have relationship problems but where neither partner is depressed. Also the problem-solving ability of *both* partners is poorer when one of them is depressed, so the couple's ability to handle both everyday problems and their relationship is reduced. Perhaps this fact is particularly important for men to understand. Exploring these interactions and the subtlety of effects, depending upon who is the sufferer of depression, is something that seems vital to develop in this chapter, for it may well be very helpful to couples trying to understand their personal predicament.

One of the important functions of a relationship is that it allows both partners an emotional closeness and support, and someone to whom each feels it is safe to disclose problems and vulnerabilities. One of the earliest and most famous of research studies of depressed women showed that the lack of a supportive relationship with a partner was associated with a greater likelihood of female depression. This is also true for men, although it is often thought that women are more needy of such closeness and support.

As one group of researchers of depression noted: 'It is a mistake for researchers to assume that women are more fragile than men.' The personal accounts bear this out, as does the fact that it may be the man who is the only partner to become depressed. Thus provision of support, both practically and emotionally, is obviously something that needs careful discussion here, as the personal accounts of the women who have experienced depression clearly show that they recognized the importance of this aspect of their relationship, or the lack of it.

Another point I wish to discuss here relates to our views of depression in men. Both men and women who are showing symptoms that we all associate with depression tend to be treated with some negativity by others. Men suffering depression, however, may experience the additional burden of being seen to be enacting a 'feminized' role. This perhaps helps to explain why it often appears that there are twice as many women who are depressed as men. Men are not encouraged to talk about their depression and tend to hide it and be stoical and 'male'. The problem for men is that because depression is seen as associated with the feminine, they can be seen as transgressing the acceptable face of 'male gender role' when depressed. In other words, the problem for a depressed man is that he is often viewed as 'bad' rather than 'sad'. Men, then, who are depressed and ask for help are particularly likely to suffer rejection by others. The stoical male who does not express his feelings or show he is depressed might actually be reacting, quite understandably, to a social reality. However, this reaction could be his worst enemy in the long run, but it is one for which he is not solely to blame.

Perhaps what is important is that everyone recognizes that depression is a medical condition in which there are changes in chemicals, called neuro-transmitters, in the brain. It is not a matter of what kind of man or woman you are, or how much of a man or woman you are; it is just a matter of each individual's biological make-up and the amount of flak life throws your way.

Research has shown, for instance, that when a large number of patients visiting the GP were assessed for being depressed, both against a standardized check-list of depressive symptomology and by their doctors, women tended to be slightly overdiagnosed (i.e. diagnosed quickly). For male patients, for every man that was diagnosed as 'depressed' by the doctor, another two were assessed as depressed by the standard criteria of the check-list, but not diagnosed as depressed by the doctor. Probably they did not tell him they felt depressed, or they did not give him sufficient clues to permit him to spot it for himself. Some researchers have also suggested that the greater expressiveness of women, both verbally and in terms of bodily and facial gesture, helps to give the clues to a doctor when assessing for depression. So there is plenty of evidence to suggest that many more men experience becoming depressed than actually appear in official figures. Although most studies suggest there is a 2:1 female to male ratio for depression, some studies suggest that the ratio is much nearer parity, and in any case, rates of male depression are rising and rates of male suicide are going through the roof.

In an original draft of this manuscript, the introduction to this chapter contained a paragraph of tremendous insight into what it could mean for a man with a female partner who was suffering post-natal depression, and I quote the author's own words after having conducted her interviews for this chapter (my italics):

> It was not an easy task as I found most of the men wanted to keep their emotions private. But as the interviews progressed, there was, surprisingly, a lot to be revealed. It was terribly sad to realize that, while their partners were suffering, they too were holding on for dear life – *trying to keep a family together, constantly 'treading on eggshells', with their own jobs to maintain, and concerns for their wives and children, not to mention their own sadness about the situation.*

The chord this paragraph strikes with the many research papers I have read is remarkable. However, at this juncture it seems sensible to invite you to read the accounts people have given and see whether some of the points made above have a resonance within the personal experiences of actual women and men. Perhaps the fact that the men's accounts are a little thinner on the ground than those of their partners already testifies to some of those points. Later, I shall return to these matters, with reference to the actual statements people have given. I hope then to go into some more helpful and interesting detail, but please now read Cara Aiken's own account and those drawn from the interviews that she conducted.

Cara

My husband never liked the baby stage. He had little if any interest in the 'babies'. He hated feeding them, never changed their nappies, and barely even noticed that they existed. The moment Georgina was born, Roo made a wall chart which was his personal countdown to our baby reaching 18 years of age – a time when perhaps we could regain some freedom. He repeated this when Tasha was born almost four years later.

I was totally responsible for our children's routines when they were babies. He didn't have a clue about feed, sleep or pooh times! He didn't know how to make up a meal, warm food up when we went out, and most certainly didn't consider nap times when fixing an outing. I could never leave either baby with him until they were at least two years old. I took the full load on my shoulders. With hindsight, after having had the two children, I should most certainly have persevered and insisted that he take a more paternal role. I didn't, and therefore by the time I was deeply depressed, I didn't have his physical or emotional support with the children.

Perhaps this is an opportune time to mention that studies are currently being carried out on the prevalence of post-natal depression in men. It is said that if a man suffers from a depression in the post-natal period, he is suffering from PND. I feel certain that my husband suffered from depression.

He could not bond with our babies, he disliked the early stages immensely, had disturbed sleep patterns even once the children were sleeping through the night, and didn't want to socialize if he could possibly avoid it. He was never given the responsibility of the children in any shape or form.

I therefore employed someone in the capacity of domestic help and child-minder, who has since become a very dear friend. I received all my help and moral support from Val, who fully understood and supported me throughout the depression. She was unfortunately not around for my first child when she was a baby, but took over my life wherever possible after the birth of Tasha. She was and still is an absolute angel in my life. I do not think I could or would have survived without her. Some people tell me that my dependency upon her gave Roo the perfect excuse for not becoming more involved. Perhaps this is true, but not to have teamed up with Val would have been a risk I could not have taken. I drew all my courage and strength from her, faced my days with her complete backing, until such time that I was able to cope alone. That took longer than I ever imagined. I do realize how very lucky I am to have had such help, and will be eternally grateful to her.

Looking back now, I realize that Roo was incredibly patient with me. He did put up with my mood swings, emotional outbursts, temper tantrums and then the total silence when I decided to go into solitary confinement! I think that a lot of husbands would have left home. But, needless to say, this was a very traumatic and sad time in my life, and one I will never forget. When I so needed the person I thought loved me most, my husband, he was not there to comfort me.

It took at least two years after the birth of my second child to realize that I did still love Roo, somewhere deep down, and that he wasn't *totally* to blame in all this mess – but just suffering, in his own way, in silence.

Roo (Cara's husband)

'To say that I hated the baby stage is an understatement. Even before we had our own babies, I was never a "baby person". I would tense up at the thought of being handed a baby to hold, even by close friends and family. I guess that by the time I knew that we were going to have our own child, I was very apprehensive. I knew that the fact was that I did not like babies, yet surely I would feel differently about my own? Wrong!

'People always try to prepare you for what it will be like when you walk through your front door with a new arrival. Yet all the preparation in the world did not prepare me for the occasion. To me it felt like a massive explosion had taken place. We had been used to our lives as a couple – and then there were three! I felt invaded. Selfishly, I began asking myself questions like "Why should I put up with the noise of a crying baby when I'm trying to sleep?", "Why should I get up in the middle of the night to feed this crying infant, surely it can wait until the morning?", and so on.

'To me it was a relief to find Cara coping so well with the situation. She would do everything – feeds, nappy changes, baths etc. I had to do nothing. As time has passed, it is very difficult for me to say whether or not I was aware of how much I neglected my duties or whether I was totally blind to it. To me, things seemed to have fallen into a very comfortable routine – *for me!* I would go to sleep at night and get up for work in the morning, while Cara did "her job" of looking after the baby. I think that I was totally unaware of the consequences this was having on Cara at the time.

'By the time Georgina was two, I began to like her, as she was now beginning to respond to me. So everything was OK! But a year or so later I was inconvenienced again by the birth of our second baby Tasha. Unknowingly I must have felt, "Well, Cara coped so well last time, she can do so again." Only this time it seemed to me that it was so much easier for Cara, as she had someone coming in every day and evening to help with Tasha. Again, to my relief, I had nothing to do with the early stages.

'By the time Tasha had reached two, I was beginning to take some interest in her, as I have said. What I didn't realize was how low Cara had got. She was suffering with what we now know was post-natal depression. I am the first to admit, now, that I was totally useless to Cara and the babies in the early years. I failed to see any signs of how my reaction to them was affecting Cara. It would be easy for me to say that I can put it down to a form of depression in myself, but deep down I think that I was being plain selfish.

'I love both my children very much indeed now, and to prove it, I threw away my "countdown to eighteen years" chart some time ago.'

Rosemary

Rosemary's husband did not help or support her when the children were born. 'My husband refused to do anything at night, pleading that he needed to be awake for work the next day. However, he would not help at the weekends either – I remember begging him to at least give our baby a bottle once every three weeks, and he would not agree. In the end I think he did so three times in the whole eight months that I breastfed her.

'He basically assumed that, being the woman, I should know how to cope. Once, when she was about five or six weeks old, I booked one night in a local hotel for myself so that I could get one night's sleep. My husband was furious and refused to let me do so. A few weeks later he was stirred into moving when he heard me shouting at 6 a.m. at the poor baby that I was going to murder her. He actually got out of bed and said that he would try to get her to go back to sleep.

'Despite my problems with the culture shock of living in Switzerland, and the fact that my husband expected me to keep house like his mother had done when we married, our relationship was still a close and basically happy one. He was as ignorant as I was as to what having children really meant. Looking back, I feel really sad about what has happened.

'I began to really enjoy my children's company after they became about seven years old, and the older they get, the better it becomes, in my experience. In a nutshell, the arrival of the children very nearly led to our divorce about two years later. The marriage was battered to breaking point – I was suffering from depression, and my husband told me that he seriously doubted that I was worth all the trouble. He never really understood what I felt, or what it is to be depressed, and this fuelled a resentment in me that I have forgiven but not forgotten.'

Jane

Jane feels that in many respects Paul supported her amazingly well. He was the only one who kept her from going under for the months before her depression was diagnosed.

'He always involved himself in the children's routine, he did everything at home and most certainly bonded with Daisy and Jacob immediately.'

Jane admits that although Paul has been very supportive, there has been a lot of tension in their relationship. 'We hadn't been going out for very long when I got pregnant with Daisy, then the nature of our relationship had to change very quickly. After Daisy's birth, Paul was really the only support I had for many months, and obviously that placed a huge burden on our relationship. I think he must have seen me as an awful burden too. I certainly wasn't the person he'd met a year earlier. I had changed from being confident and assertive, to needing constant reassurance, just to get through the day.

'Paul was having to adjust to his new role as a father, hold down a full-time job and still work part-time towards a degree. My depression obviously made things even harder, and as a result Paul started to drink heavily, and eventually had to seek help from an alcoholic adviser. In the end, he managed to get the amount he was drinking under control, and I appreciate now that he was using alcohol as a way to escape, if only temporarily, from the problems we were having. If I had not been ill, Paul would have been well too. Even though I am well now, our relationship is only just beginning to recover.'

Paul (Jane's partner)

'How did I feel when Jane was ill? Crap, because I couldn't cope. Pushed out, because Jane devoted so much time to Daisy and less to me. Scared, because Jane had considered smothering Daisy. Afraid for my health and for Jane's stability.

'I lost my confidence; I lost my sex drive; as time went on, I almost lost the will to live. I found it increasingly difficult to cope. I was looking after Jane; looking after Daisy; trying to hold down a job; halfway through a five-year degree course. I subsequently stopped looking after me.

'One of the features of Jane's illness was the constant hand-washing. I think she single-handedly kept "Wet-Wipes TM" in business. Jane would wash her hands whenever she saw a word – like the word "death" – or a place – like a funeral parlour – that upset her. This meant that she would not read the paper, or would travel on such a route as would bypass a certain building, so that she would not put herself into the position of reading about or seeing the thing that upset her.

'This was obviously tiring for Jane; the effect it had on me was to grind me down. Every time Jane felt endangered, she would ask for my reassurance that because she had seen something that upset her, it would not harm Daisy. Each time I replied that it would not; but each time I felt less and less sure that Jane believed me. The constant requests were like demands on my time. I began to feel that the only way I could get away was to be at work. Even there, though, Jane would telephone me (perhaps around six or seven times a day) to ask for my reassurance.

'I began to feel I needed time for myself. So I began to go for a drink after work, so that I could summon up the necessary Dutch courage to go home. And as Jane worsened, so did I and my drink problem.

'Jane would tell me that when Daisy was sleeping, she imagined she was dead. This made her "happy", in that she was so convinced that Daisy was going to die anyway that she thought this was the kindest way for her to go. She also considered smothering Daisy because she could no longer cope with her own illness. This was a way of controlling Daisy's death.

'I felt happier when Jane began to receive professional help, to at least know that she was not going mad. But again, I felt pushed out. The psychiatrist at the hospital to whom she was referred, the Queen Elizabeth Psychiatric Hospital in Birmingham, often wanted to see her alone.

'I could understand that, first and foremost, they wanted to get to the bottom of Jane's illness; what I could not understand was why they did not want to know how I felt, how I was coping. Selfish, yes; but I felt I needed to talk to someone too, to tell them how I felt. I was hurting too. The QEPH attempted to establish a men's support group for the partners of women suffering from post-natal depression. This never got off the ground, due to the lack of interest from the men it was designed to help. I could not talk to Jane – it would only burden her more. I could not talk to my mother, since my relationship with her was strained, to say the least. Work colleagues were insensitive – most of them had the "pull yourself together" attitude. I was turning to alcohol for solace. Assignments had deadlines. Money was tight. I couldn't cope.

'I eventually sought help through the staff counsellor at work. After a number of meetings with her, I was referred to an alcohol advisory service. Slowly, I felt able to hold it together. I reduced my alcohol intake.

'I moved into a different department at work. My wages increased. I still had a daughter. OK, so I still also had an awful mother, and Jane and I had come close to splitting on a number of occasions, but things were slowly working out.

'So how are things now? I've completed my degree – 2:1, a grade I am really proud of, considering Jane was ill for three of the five years. I've been promoted at work, so while there are more problems there (in terms of increased responsibility) I am more financially secure. I have two wonderful children: Daisy, now four, and Jacob, aged two. I'm still working on the mother–son relationship.

'And Jane and I? I think that Jane's illness took something away from our relationship. That is not meant to be harsh on Jane. All it means is that I see us as having a brother–sister relationship, where we have a mutual need to look after the children. Will anything return? Who knows? But the best thing to come out of all of it is two lovely and loving children. And that is something to be thankful for.'

Julie

Julie views her husband Michael as what most women would call the perfect husband and daddy. 'He donned the housework pinny and the nursemaid's hat and kept the husband's head. If only I could have worn all those faces and coped as well.' Julie feels that Michael sailed through it all at first, leaving her 'gawping' behind. He bonded with Sarah immediately. Julie received a lot of support from him, both physically and mentally. 'But of course there were times when he just lost his patience, didn't understand and shut himself off from me.'

Michael (Julie's husband)

'Our daughter was a very wanted baby. My wife and I were both over the moon once she was pregnant. The pregnancy went fairly well.

'I hated hearing her spill her insides into the toilet every day, knowing there was nothing I could do to help, but really enjoyed sharing the experience of her pregnancy, cuddling the growing bump, feeling the first movements etc.

'Sex was intermittent. I felt conscious in the early months that I might be hurting Julie or the baby, and later Julie felt very conscious of her size, felt uncomfortable and tired, but we still remained close.

'As you can imagine, I was totally shell-shocked when a while after the birth she became Jekyll and Hyde. Of course she had always been moody once a month, something we men expect (but never get used to), but she totally changed. While still on maternity leave she became much more tired than normal, went totally off sex and was very "touchy". At first I understood a little – after all, she had just had a baby, been stitched in the nether regions and had her hormones totally messed up. I tried not to pressure her, helped out with Sarah and the house as much as I could and took her out, but things just got worse. She was very short-tempered with me, shouting one minute and in floods of tears the next, screaming at Sarah as if her crying was causing her pain. I tried to be patient, calm and understanding, but sometimes I just couldn't understand.

'I was very protective of my daughter and did criticize Julie at times for losing her patience so easily. After all, she was only a baby and couldn't fend for herself. Little did I know that Julie felt she couldn't look after herself at that time, either, and my comments just made it worse.

'I think we all felt unloved at some time, and I just had to put up a brick wall at times to keep sane.

'I didn't realize just how bad Julie was until one night when Sarah was about two and a half months old. I was cuddling up to my daughter while she took her late-night bottle, and Julie was, I thought, in bed asleep. As I crept back downstairs I overheard a blubbering wife on the phone in the kitchen. She was talking to the doctor, checking if she would be all right after taking just a few too many tablets.

'I just couldn't believe it. "WHY?" I cried, but through the curtain of tears she just sobbed, "I don't know, I just don't know." I hugged her so hard she almost cracked and I ached with pain. The realization that I could have lost my wife frightened me, and I didn't even know she felt so bad. The doctor helped me understand a little, explaining that post-natal depression didn't need a reason to appear, and that Julie wouldn't know why she felt how she did. He gave her some anti-depressants which I had to keep, as well as keeping an eye on her. She felt like a child who wasn't trusted and I felt – well, I don't really know how I felt.

'The next few months were hard. Julie felt ashamed of what she nearly did, and still felt like a worthless mother and wife, no matter what I said or did. I loved her dearly, but I started to feel that I couldn't cope, and couldn't talk to her about it, either, which caused a barrier between us. I have to admit that at times I felt totally cheesed off. I know it wasn't her fault, how she was acting, but I just didn't understand and found it hard to have enough patience for her and Sarah. I just wanted my wife back! One minute she wanted a cuddle, the next she pushed me away – what *did* she want? She needed bucketfuls of sleep, so I tended to take the bulk of caring for Sarah. Julie did have to take a short time off sick from work, but I was working, so the extra hours I was taking on at home and coping with emotional volcanoes did cause a strain. I did feel resentful at times – not nice to admit – but again, I couldn't help it.

'I never stopped loving Julie, but as I said, I did have to distance myself from her at times for self-preservation, for the sake of my mental state. The depression went on for a long time, slowly easing, and once I started to see signs of my old wife appearing, I was hopeful. Unfortunately she had a relapse, went back on the anti-depressants, came off a few months later, felt great for a few months, but then had another relapse after pressure at work. She doesn't realize when her symptoms are returning, though, and it takes a lot of nagging to get her to see she has a problem and go to the doctor. She is so stubborn, and hates to feel she needs help. She gets worse before she gets help, which tests my patience to the limit. She is still on anti-depressants after two years, but is improving a lot again.

'I can't help wondering if it will ever end. They say two years isn't a long time to have post-natal depression, it can last longer (heaven forbid). But it feels like a lifetime to me, and probably to Julie as well. I know she feels guilty for being how she has been, and I feel guilty for thinking and saying the sometimes hurtful and unhelpful things I have. No matter how much you care for someone, I don't think anything can prepare you for depression, and you just can't understand something you haven't suffered from yourself. It's not like a broken leg or having surgery – it's something you can't see, and you can't help wondering if it's all in the mind sometimes.

'I know "Pull yourself together" is the worst possible thing you can say, but at times you want to shake them and tell them just that.

'Through all of this I was having mixed feelings too – hurt, anger, concern, frustration and isolation. At times it wasn't easy having enough patience for our daughter and Julie as well, so I may have appeared a little hard sometimes, which must have hurt Julie. As she still isn't as well as she should be, and as it has been going on for some time, she has been referred to a psychiatrist. I must admit that I wasn't too sure about this at first, as I am worried that bringing up her past might just make matters worse. Julie is also frightened, and doesn't know what to expect. She worries about official notes being made about her, where these notes will go, and what they're used for. The stigma of seeing a psychiatrist worries her a lot.

'She and we can't go on like this for ever, though, so she is going to go ahead and see what happens. I want my wife back and of course our sex life, something that has always been good, which makes it even harder for me to cope with now. I have wondered at times if she has gone off me or found someone else, but I do know that she really loves me. She says she just can't help feeling like she does. She tries her best, but it's not really something she can control. Her pre-period times are still worse than they used to be, but I'm trying to bite my tongue a bit more when she snaps and she's trying not to growl as much. If this doesn't work, I just take cover!'

Pippa

Reflecting on her experience, Pippa is adamant that, without her husband John's support, she would never have got through the labour and birth. She feels sure that he felt included and wanted throughout.

When John is at home, he will take Callum from her whether she needs him to or not. And then she can go shopping or visit the PND support group. 'Although the group has a crèche, I can hear him if he cries – it is so off-putting, it's distressing.' John has always done as much as he can. He will do what he thinks is best for Callum, although he doesn't always have the same ideas as Pippa.

'This is still a sticking-point for us – differences of opinion. He is very involved in Callum's routine, and bonded with him long before I did. I need John to help and to be there for Callum. He copes well, but also gets ill-tempered at times and gets back-ache (join the club, boy!). We have separate duties in our house and try to help each other out – it is very much a partnership, a joint affair. We both put the effort in.' Although John has at times had some self-doubt, Pippa saw him as being very confident with Callum. He would stimulate him more and always seemed to be more comfortable with him. 'He had and still has the knack of giving Callum different things to play with – he has a different approach. He gave him a plastic lid to play with and Callum seemed fascinated by it – and it held his attention. That was something I wouldn't have thought of.'

In Pippa's opinion, men don't suffer from this depression. 'They don't have the hormones going mad inside – they don't get the peaks and troughs. They just have to watch us. Perhaps they suffer it in a different way. They also don't always know what to do, as much as we don't know what to do. But I've been too busy having my own depression to think about his!'

John (Pippa's husband)

John feels that he did as much as he possibly could to help Pippa. 'In the very beginning, I wasn't taking as much of the burden because I was spending a lot of that time flying around buying all the necessary baby equipment. That was something we didn't know about – we didn't even have a Moses basket for the first few weeks, and so either Pippa or myself had to hold Callum all the time!

'I was involved in Callum's routine from the start but it took until he was six months old for me to realize that his routine was inviolate. I had to go along with *his* timetable – that was very hard to cope with. He had *his* routine and *I* had to work within that to accommodate *him*. I didn't really bond with Callum until he was about four months old. If we had had a really bad day or night and someone from the hospital had knocked on the door and offered to take him back, I would have thought, we've done our bit, proved we're not good at this, and would have said, "We have enjoyed this trial period, but you can have him back now!" After four months, that feeling went away. Now I couldn't be without him.'

At times, John did feel a tiny bit pushed out by Pippa. 'The baby took up so much of Pippa's time, and he was receiving all of her attention. I never felt pushed out by the baby himself because I know Pippa and I are his "best friends" at the moment. We have been since he was born – if we can't accommodate his needs, the feelings that he engenders in us, then it's a failing on our part. I have to rationalize and do the best I can for him.'

In the very early stages, John thought that a certain amount of bringing up a child should come naturally to a woman. 'These thoughts were in despite of Pippa's protestations that she had never done any of this before, and that she didn't have a clue what to do. I had grown up with small children around me, whom I helped to bring up to a certain extent. I had experienced feeding a baby and changing a nappy – I was familiar with the physical presence of children. I realize that this was pretty naïve of me, looking back on it – and even a bit condescending. But I think that I viewed her as somebody who really could cope innately.'

At one time, in the early stages, John had a certain feeling of detachment, not depression. 'I was fascinated by all the baby equipment in the early days and read every pram brochure about. (I could name any pram at 50 yards, and could tell you if it was this year's or last year's model!) It all became an obsession for a while, researching into what pram etc. we should buy. I became so absorbed in the equipment side of things, that how the bigger picture was going to look was only a slowly dawning realization. Eventually, reality took hold, as opposed to the nonsense about the equipment.'

When Callum was six months old, John began to feel a lack of confidence in dealing with him. 'Callum had become very attached to Pippa, and this knocked my confidence. Pippa was more confident by this time and Callum was able to get closer to her emotionally. I was no longer getting the feedback from him. It may have been a developmental phase that he was going through, and, the health visitor reminded me, more of his time was being spent with Pippa while I was out and about. I wasn't getting that "face-to-face" time with Callum which was what was needed. I had been working long hours and getting home late. Then, when work slowed down, things improved. This wasn't anything too serious – just a few little mind games my brain had been playing on me.'

John's image of Pippa was changing all the time. 'I realized that she was finding it all very difficult. I do feel that Pippa is coping better now, and I always did think that she was coping better than she thought she was. Callum has always been well fed and properly looked after. However bad she seems to feel, she has always managed to put him first, and has kept him as he should be. He has thrived and put on so much weight in the first few months that I'm sure no baby could have been looked after better. A bit later on, at five months, when Pippa was diagnosed as having post-natal depression by the health visitor, I saw her as somebody who was just plain scared about the whole thing. Once or twice at that time when I saw her looking after Callum, it would have been obvious to a blind man that she wasn't really confident in what she was doing.

'I could actually feel the physical manifestation of fear within her, and it made me think that I'd been blithely barrelling along. I mean, OK, I'd known she was having difficulties, but she had seemed to be doing fine and it made me realize that, hey, maybe this is not such a rosy picture as I seem to be painting in my head.

'Now Callum is eight months old, and Pippa's a lot more confident. She has found that her confidence has been boosted by the fact that Callum responds a lot more. She is getting some feedback from him and finds that gratifying. She's obviously lacking confidence in herself, but I see her ability and confidence with Callum improving greatly.

'She seems much more at ease, if you look back to the first few weeks, and she has improved even more in the last month or so. Callum is always so happy to see her. If there is any fear left in her own belief in her ability to look after him, he doesn't pick up on that at all. I am sure that it is a case of accepting that you don't know what you are doing, and getting used to that feeling.'

Physically, John had no problems at all in dealing with Callum. 'I was used to babies and was not afraid of "breaking him in half". I have dealt with him from morning to night, all day, on my own – it's not a problem. And I've got round to the idea of slotting into "his" routine. But there have been times when I've had Callum all day, realized it was almost 7 p.m., and felt relief in the fact that Pippa would be back in two minutes.'

Callum relates differently to John than he does to Pippa. 'Callum seems more "pally" with Pippa, responds better to her and is more familiar with her. Pippa spends more time with him. It might just be a "male to female" thing.'

Says John, 'My role in our household is chief cook, bottle-washer, driver and back-massager! Before Callum, we each had our own jobs in the house, we each had a departmental responsibility! That has changed. Pippa also thinks of me as the cavalry coming in the front door to give her a respite from Callum!

'I do feel that the partner who spends more time out at work is perhaps not quite so nurturing, but more adventurous with the child. I also believe in bringing the outside world to him, and do just that each day.

'I honestly feel that I could cope well with the baby alone from when he was quite young and that I helped Pippa through a difficult time, but I wasn't awfully good at breastfeeding!'

Laura

Although Laura and Russell were engaged and married within months, Laura most definitely believes she found her 'soul-mate'. 'Russell understood me while I was going through my depression – totally and completely – although there was a time when he admitted that he thought I would never come through my psychosis. I think if it had been just a depression, he could have coped with it, but the problem was never knowing what he would be visiting. He used to make jokes and take a rather light-hearted view at times, which infuriated me. "It couldn't be all doom and gloom every day," he once remarked – he was right.

'He managed to hold down his job and care part-time for Hannah while I was ill. I will always marvel at his calmness when dealing with particularly stressful situations. Russell has always had a fantastic relationship with Hannah and she is a real "daddy's girl" – he loves that.

'Our relationship has shown tremendous strength throughout this whole ordeal and only fuels my earlier belief that we truly are "soul-mates".'

Gail

'My husband was a total rock, and he is still by my side, which proves what kind of man he truly is. I remember telling him to go and that no one would blame him. He just replied that he married me for better or for worse and through sickness and in health, and that I had always been there for him. His love for me was so strong, it kept us together and I know it will never die.'

Gail's husband

Gail's husband felt helpless throughout her illness and didn't know what to do. He too was going through hell, but people seemed to disregard his feelings. He just wanted his wife back and never doubted for a minute that she would return to him. He was willing to pay any amount of money to get her better.

Jenny

Jenny's husband initially mentioned the possibility of her terminating her third pregnancy, which she had no intention of doing. He was almost 50 years old, and Jenny feels that as he worked so hard, he was having thoughts of an easier time with early retirement possibly in the offing.

He was with Jenny for the birth. 'As usual, he was very calm and supportive, but significantly, when he found out that the baby was another girl, he very quickly decided to go home as he wanted to go back to bed! He didn't even wait for the statutory cup of tea. I was very upset about this. It was as if now that he had done his bit, it was over to me, and for the next five years I would do all the work. To be fair to him, I had done the lion's share with the first two children but had thoroughly enjoyed it, quite easily monopolizing the care of both children. This time, however, I felt different.

'I also felt resentful because he took so little time off, and actually went away for a night in the first couple of weeks when I felt I couldn't cope. He had cancelled trips to see some rugby matches just before I had the baby, however, so I felt I couldn't complain too much!

'My depression never really put a strain on our relationship, as the way I was was so very different from my normal self. My husband didn't demand very much of me and realized that I just had to go through it, and he was generally supportive and let me be. He did organize an extra holiday when the baby was about a year old, which was very nice and helped a little.

'I appreciated that he was so undemanding, although he could have supported me better around the actual birth, and in the first weeks. I think what happened to me surprised him as much as it surprised me.'

Sarah

Once at home, Michael did help Sarah with the practical aspects. 'He fed me well, cleared up, and generally looked after the home. I was not well, and I feel as though I never got out of bed for a long, long time. But even with Michael at home, I still felt terribly lonely. Michael was there constantly, but not with me or Matthew. He was devastated by the sudden responsibility of our baby. I think that, psychologically, he just shut himself off. He would disappear to a different part of the house, closing doors behind him. This was his way of gaining isolation – he was looking after his own needs while I was left with the baby. Michael's attitude to the baby crying so much was "What will the neighbours think?" He didn't worry about *why* Matthew was crying, or how this was affecting me. I felt angry about his attitude, which made me feel the need for me and Matthew to become "invisible" to the world.'

Veritee

Barry never realized the intensity of Veritee's illness. He was away at sea for long stretches and couldn't support her during a lot of the extremely difficult periods.

'Having read what Barry has written I was really happy to see how much he trusted me while it was all going on. Trust is really important in a relationship, and I was very scared, at the time, that my fears that I would harm Caja would destroy the trust and respect he had for me. However, I am overwhelmed that he did not realize just how bad things were for me.

'He did not seem to realize the extent of the months of depression, after the birth, when I spent hours alone, absolutely desperate. At this particular point, I might not have wanted to harm Caja consciously, but I was definitely off my tree! I can remember waking up one morning after a particularly stormy night, convinced that the end of the world had come! It was so quiet, as I live up a lonely lane, and I thought I was the only person left. I remember wondering if it would be best to kill Caja and commit suicide now, as we would probably die horrible lonely deaths from starvation if I didn't. I actually had to go to a meeting at work that morning for the first time since Caja was born.

'This might have saved us, as I operated on autopilot, and went to the meeting anyway. Once I'd got on the main road, I realized that it had been my imagination. Barry was away at that time but I did tell him about it. *To think that even my partner did not notice that he was living with someone who was mentally ill bordering on the psychotic!* He was not the only one who noticed nothing. At that particular meeting, I remember saying, "This morning I thought the end of the world had come." I wonder what they thought I meant?

'At that time I was obsessed with the environment and was convinced that I had only brought my little girl into the world to die young from some environmental disaster. I was expecting this all the time, and the fact that there were many violent storms that year that I had never seen the like of in my life made me all the more convinced that I was right. I often used to say to Caja over and over again that I was sorry I had done what I had done to her – brought her into a world which was dying. I suppose these thoughts were so like the thoughts of some fervent environmentalists that no one noticed.

'At this point I also had this peculiar feeling that I couldn't see properly. I obviously could, as I was driving and reading, but I used to say to Caja and Barry, "Everything would be all right if only I could see properly." Barry obviously did not notice this at all.

'I did get over this psychotic stage when Caja was seven months, which was helped by my going back to work, as I was now being confronted with reality every day. But I find it astounding that Barry did not notice – nor did my friends or the health visitor, doctor or even my father who was living in Cornwall at that time. Surely he knew well enough? It was not as if I did not tell anyone. I would tell everyone who would listen about the obsessions and a lot of other peculiar things I thought at that time. I used to go to the mother and toddler group and break down and tell them. Eventually they delegated two nice women to talk to me to tell me I couldn't come any more if I didn't stop breaking down and saying the things I did, as it might affect the children.

'I did say some awful things about how I hated being a mother and how I hated young children and couldn't see anything good at all about having a baby, and how I never wanted children in the first place and wished I'd never had them. I used to get angry with the other mothers, who appeared to be enjoying parenting their children. My life was such hell and I resented the other women for not finding it so hard. I would shout and swear at Caja in front of them. I used to swear violently a lot, and many of the women had led sheltered lives in rural Cornwall and found it very offensive, but I could not help myself.

'I do not blame the women at the group for their reaction. It is just an example of how we are conditioned to shy away from raw emotion and push it away. If my husband and family were not prepared to deal with it, how could I expect young mothers (most at least ten years younger than me) to deal with a middle-aged woman who was always screaming and crying?

'At work it was only later that anyone questioned my sanity, and by that time I was a lot better. They only started to worry because they found out that I was involved with the Social Services and because I started to cry and break down at work because of that.

'I found that I just could not be in a group where feelings were talked about, because my feelings were so overwhelming that I would cry and cry and get angry whenever feelings of almost any kind were discussed. Obviously very out of order for a youth worker whose working life consists of being in groups where feelings are discussed! They could not help but notice, yet I got little understanding or help – just the added threat that I would lose my job on top of everything else.

'All this time Barry still did not seem to notice it as much as the people I worked with, yet I was constantly on the edge. Perhaps he was so used to me by this time that he felt it was all quite normal. After all, despite my outbursts and the strange things I was saying, I did carry on caring for Caja and Barry, doing all the housework, looking after all the animals when he was away, and still going to work. He might have seen it as my way of relieving the strain. But it wasn't. I was truly on the edge and I feel lucky to have survived it without harming myself, Caja or someone else.

'I cannot help but think that Barry did not want to see just how bad I really was, as then he would have had to face the possibility of leaving his job, or even of me having to give up my job. Either would have meant we would have lost the house we lived in, probably by repossession, as we do need both wages to remain here. If Barry had registered how ill I was, he would either have had to risk this, or stayed on at sea and lived with the fact that his wife was mentally ill. He then would have had to cope with how he felt about that. Therefore, he had no option but to trust me. I do wish he would have taken a little of this responsibility on board himself.

'Because he did not register how bad I was, it meant that I had to face the whole thing entirely alone. I knew by the time I started to feel scared of hurting Caja just how ill I actually was. I could not seem to get this through to Barry, which made me think that he thought I was moaning about nothing and putting it all on. Also, after the incident with Social Services, I was scared to let anyone official know how ill and desperate I had become. I was so scared that I would never get better, and wanted to kill myself for Caja's and Barry's sake. Yet most of the time I had a partner who acted as if there was nothing, out of the ordinary, wrong.

'Even at times when I would scream and cry and tell him how desperate I was, although he would seem a bit upset at the time, the next day he acted as if nothing had happened. All he would seem to be worried about was the expense of having a family, and living in this house, which would put more pressure on me to keep working as I desperately did not want to be responsible for losing the home we had fought to make. This made me feel even more responsibility for destroying my family's lives.

'I felt so alone throughout my whole illness. I could not even get over to my partner how ill I was and, in turn, help him to give me the support I needed. Even his recognition of the severity of my illness would have been a support, as then I would have felt it was a problem we were facing together. As it was, it felt like *my* problem, and his problems were of my making too. I was responsible for us having moved to this house and the expense it brought, for having had a baby and that expense, for not being well enough to get a full-time job yet needing decent clothes for work, and having to run two cars so I could work.

'All of this makes it seem like we do not have a good relationship, yet we do. On the plus side, Barry has always trusted, loved and respected me. I am free to make my own decisions in life, and I do not have a partner who has any expectations of what a wife should do. By this I mean I am not expected to be home for him or have a meal on the table every night. I rarely go out, as there is nowhere else I'd rather be than at home with Caja and Barry. When he is home he will look after Caja all the time if I have other things to do, and he does not resent my time spent elsewhere.

'We share most things in life and make together all the decisions that affect us both. It is just unfortunate that we could not share the burden of my illness, as this was very lonely. But I understand that he probably could not cope with it any other way.'

Barry (Veritee's husband)

'I was worried when Veritee was ill during her pregnancy, but not much more than normal, as she often seemed to feel ill at that time. For some reason I never really thought that anything would go wrong with the pregnancy or that we would not have a healthy baby at the end of it. Although given Veritee's age and the smallness of Caja, I suppose we were lucky.

'Veritee did complain about having to cope with the animals while I was away, and I worried about that. However, when I suggested getting rid of them to make life easier, she said no, they were needed to make living on a farm worthwhile, and that was why we bought the farm in the first place. So I just felt at a loss as to what to do – I was looking at practical ways to make life easier for Veritee, but they were all rejected, which was very frustrating.

'When I heard she had been admitted to hospital, I realized how dangerous high blood pressure was. It took me over two days to get home from a ship in the North Sea (I had to be helicoptered off and I have a fear of this and avoid it if I can). I was worrying all the way home. However, when I did get home, her blood pressure had dropped a bit and I thought everything was OK. The next few days were OK and then I left the hospital for about two hours to get something to eat. When I came back Veritee had been induced.

'From then on it was a nightmare, with one cock-up after another. It was unbelievable that I had to wheel Veritee up to the operating room for a Caesarean myself as there were no portering staff available. I also had to lift her on and off trolleys, with her suffering pain at every movement. In addition, there was no anaesthetist on duty despite the fact she had been in pain for several hours.

'I was so relieved when it was all over and I was given Caja to hold. At this point I thought everything was fine, and even though Caja went to special care I thought that all the problems were over. I did not really register that an emergency Caesarean was quite a major operation even though, when I next saw Veritee, she had numerous drains and drips attached to her. It was all so new to me and you hear of women having Caesareans all the time. I thought it was routine that they took pictures of Caja, and did not realize it was done for Veritee, so that she could register the fact that she had had a live baby. I took the picture home with me to show my friends.

'I did not have a lot of choice about going back to work after the birth. Also, I was not having a lot to do with Caja at this time. Veritee was either sleeping with her, or holding her, or breastfeeding her. I did change a few nappies. There was a couple living in a caravan about 30 feet from the house at the time, so I did not feel I was leaving her completely alone.

'I was really annoyed with the Social Services. We were doing everything we could to get Caja to eat, and they were no help at all, especially after Caja had been admitted to the hospital. All they could get her to eat was ice-cream, and she came back to us weighing less than when she went in. I was away for all of this. As for the home help [family aide]! – all she seemed to do was turn up at mealtimes and check that we were feeding her properly, as they obviously couldn't. She did nothing practical to help us. We had told them we were feeding her – didn't they believe us? We could have done with some practical help at this time when I was at sea, so that Veritee could have a rest from the worry of looking after an underweight child, but they only seemed to be interested in checking up on us, not helping us.

'As for the case conference, I told Veritee to try to get it postponed so that I could attend, as she knew how the system worked. I think it is completely wrong that they would not do this. They went ahead and held a conference about my child, at a time when I had no chance of attending. They did not seem to understand that I could not get off the ship for anything short of a death or severe illness in the family. If the ship is left without a second engineer out at sea, it cannot work and the firm stands to lose thousands of pounds from one man's absence on that contract.

'I suppose they thought that if it was important to me, I would have attended. But there was no way I could have got my firm to helicopter me off at such short notice. I was due back in a week anyway – surely they could have rearranged it for then. Veritee did explain that I could not get back, but all they said was that they were all busy people and they would hold it without both of us if they had to!

'The problem with the knives and Veritee being frightened that she might harm Caja started when Caja was about two years old, just after the case conference and all the other problems with the Social Services. Their involvement did so much harm to someone who was already suffering from depression. I always trusted Veritee not to harm Caja. It never really entered my head that she would do anything, and I think that throwing the knives away just made her feel safer. After Christmas, having failed the exams of the course the company had sent me on, I started coming home only every other weekend, which did not help Veritee. I could support her less than when I was at sea. But I always trusted her to look after Caja at all times.

'I would have nothing whatsoever to do with Social Services again, and would not tell anyone to go to them whatever the problem, after what they did to us. This is despite the fact that Veritee still works closely with the Social Services and is involved in referring children to them from time to time.'

Dr Malcolm George concludes:

Having read the accounts, I am sure the issue of how supportive husbands or partners are to their partners was a crucial matter to the women (and to some of their men). It is evident that in some of the cases, a female post-natal depression seemed to be almost predictable even before the birth, which itself was just the last straw.

Depression can easily have deep-seated roots in the adversities that are part of life experience, so that if a depression does strike, considerable expert help may be needed, including talking the past through, before the depression resolves. However, as I said previously, research shows that a lack of closeness in a relationship is one of the key predictive factors for depression in women, even without pregnancy. Although the accounts obviously do not go into all the details, it can be surmised that even before the birth there was what might be called 'relationship distress' in some of the cases in which post-natal depression ensued. It is, I am sure, not lost on anyone that a distressed relationship before birth is hardly likely to improve with the arrival of the baby. Neither is it worth discussing, for the same reason, the male partner who is totally unsupportive and selfish – or even worse, abusive. Both would be a potential breeding ground for depressive symptomology.

Research shows that the support male partners give during pregnancy may be a vital element contributing to whether depression occurs post-natally. It has been found that pregnant women's expectations of the support they will need when their baby is born involve both practical and emotional support. They wish their partner and others to provide practical help, but they judge the emotional support their partner can give to be the more vital and important.

It certainly does not take an academic to say it for most men to realize that their partner needs emotional support. Perhaps the problem from a male perspective is not the failure to realize this, but a degree of uncertainty as to exactly what emotional support to be giving. To cover this comprehensively would take a book in itself and I am not going to try, except to say that often relationship breakdown is not just to do with negative relationship aspects but with absence of positives as well.

Research has identified that there is a key item of support needed during pregnancy, which is essentially emotional. In particular, women want to have their expectancies during pregnancy of the level of practical support they might need once the baby is born validated by their male partners. Bearing in mind that pregnancy and childbirth are a time of potentially great vulnerability for women, this is absolutely reasonable. It is knowing that their male partner agrees with them and supports them in their expectations of what should happen, or what might be needed, and is committed to seeing that at the appropriate time this will happen, that gives the much needed emotional support. Ironically, the research also shows that when push came to shove, it did not actually matter so much whether it was the men themselves who provided the expected practical support.

What really mattered to the wives was that their partner had upheld their expectations and that the practical support was available from someone, although not necessarily from him. So perhaps the lesson for men is that giving emotional support, and getting that right, is a way of helping their partner which will help prevent her from becoming post-natally depressed in the first place. The added bonus is that when the baby is born, the practical level of support a man can actually provide will be less of an issue as long as that support is available somehow and somewhere.

Indeed, it may well take some of the heat off husbands and male partners themselves, and lessen their own problems of coping and 'holding on for dear life'. If it prevents a man's partner becoming post-natally depressed, it is going to be well worth the effort for him alone.

In a sense, from the accounts we have read in this book, we may wonder whether in some cases the complaints about lack of practical support voiced by the women were really just heartfelt complaints about the lack of emotional support their men gave as husbands or partners, not just as fathers. It is perhaps not hard to spot this in practice. And it is an interesting consequence of this reasoning that a man who provides oodles of practical support, but does not get the emotional support package at all right, is surprised when his partner still becomes depressed and criticizes him for not giving her support.

His efforts, though commendable in one sense, are misplaced, and one can perhaps see in this scenario the elements that lead to both partners ending up more stressed and depressed. In what may seem a cruel twist, some men who give little practical support are actually not seen as unsupportive by their partner. They do give just the right *emotional* support she needs, and so the practicalities of life between the couple – who does what – are just not an issue. So our discussion of the role of husbands or partners in women's post-natal depression might well be at the heart of the problem. Male partners may be a key element to helping prevent PND occurring, or a very important part of the road to recovery, or the absence of it.

I want to move on now and look at male partners and the problems they may face in coping, when their wife or partner has become depressed post-natally for whatever reason. Reading the accounts myself, I was repeatedly drawn to one paragraph of Paul's experience of it all: 'I lost my confidence; I lost my sex drive; as time went, I almost lost the will to live. I found it increasingly difficult to cope. I was looking after Jane; looking after Daisy; trying to hold down a job; halfway through a five-year degree course. *I subsequently stopped looking after me*' (my italics). These words are so powerful in their despair. Paul was, in the male vernacular, 'totally up shit creek without a paddle'.

His sense of isolation is all too evident and his determination to do his best as a man, as partner for Jane and father for Daisy, no matter the cost to him, heroic. His phrases are prophetic – loss of confidence, no sex drive, loss of will to live, difficulty in coping. Loss of sex drive can be a give-away complaint of the depressed man, but it seems that Paul's despair went further and got close to suicidal. I wonder if he ever told anyone this at the time?

As I said earlier, it is known that a close relationship is supportive and protective against depression. This is true for men, not just for women, and in the accounts of both wives and husbands it is evident that a partner's depression robbed some men of emotional support. It is instructive perhaps to relate that a British study of post-natally depressed women and their partners found that when these mothers and their babies were taken into a mother and baby care unit, a sizeable number of their partners were suddenly found to be in need of help. Suddenly these men were seen to be very depressed themselves.

It is easily imaginable, from what Paul describes, that a man feeling as he did, and clearly suffering himself, would be devastated by the loss of his partner into hospital; it would confirm his thinking that he had not coped. He, as a man, partner and father, had not lived up to what he thought he should have been able to do for his family and still manage to cope all on his own. To repeat the author's original observations: such men are *holding on for dear life – trying to keep a family together, constantly "treading on eggshells", with their own jobs to maintain, concerns for their wives and children, not to mention their own sadness about the situation.*'

It is often the case that men have far fewer people around them, than women have, to whom they feel able to open up and confide their worries. Women are said to have larger support networks than men. Clearly, in some of the accounts we have read, the women did *not* have large support networks around them and were heavily reliant on their partners for support. However, for a woman, even having a large support network can be a double-edged sword. It provides support, but the other members of the network need support as well. It can happen that a number of members are needy of support at the same time. So women may both benefit and be disadvantaged by having larger networks of confidants than men. Many men, on the other hand, have only one confidant – their partner. That can be a little onerous for the female partner, but it can also be a disaster for men.

When a man's partner is depressed, it may well be that the form his own sadness at the situation takes is not to mention it or not accept any emotional support even if he does. Taking all the other factors into account, it is not hard to see that a depressed female partner constitutes a risk for a man becoming depressed himself.

Men, however, tend to cope with feelings of low mood in a different and sometimes more successful manner than women do. Men find ways of distracting themselves from their depressive feelings. It might be throwing themselves completely into their work, or disappearing to the sports club or just down to the pub. It is a technique that can work, but one that often has hidden dangers for men. For instance, the pub can be the path to a much increased alcohol consumption in an attempt to blot out the distress felt. Unfortunately, this last recourse just exacerbates the problem and may make the man's depressive feelings worse in the long run. Paul, in his account, certainly seems to have realized his mistake. Of course, such male distractive behaviour is often not appreciated by partners, and in several of the narratives above the man seems to be using a distraction to save himself pain. Unfortunately, at the same time he is viewed unfavourably by his partner.

This is what I might term a male dilemma over depression and depressive feelings – either men tend to try and deny their sense of gloom, or they are seen to be depressed, but either way they can easily be seen by their partners as behaving 'badly', not just 'sadly'.

The problem for the man is that using his ability to distract himself as a technique to help his partner – i.e. by distracting her from her distress – may not work because of women's tendency to dwell on their feelings of low mood and ruminate about them. Perhaps a little more insight, on both partners' parts, into the way they themselves, and the other one, react and operate, could provide the understanding to allow the couple to come together and support each other, rather than move more apart as a result of their own separate feelings of distress.

Another aspect of men's way of trying to cope, as Paul's account seems to suggest, arises out of the 'not to mention' factor. I wonder how many of the male partners went, for instance, to their own GP and said, 'My wife has post-natal depression and I am finding it really difficult to cope, looking after her, the baby, myself, etc., etc., and I think I am depressed and need some help.' As Paul so aptly remarks, 'I subsequently stopped looking after me.' It is known that men with depression (as with other illnesses) are less likely than women to seek help or go to a doctor. In the case of a man with a depressed wife or partner, with the possibility of himself also becoming depressed, it is quite easy to see how Paul's deterioration occurred – without help or support for himself, he also became a casualty and so would have been even less effective in providing support for Jane and Daisy.

Also evident in the men's accounts is the fact that they often felt excluded, and perhaps in some of the women's accounts…well, shall we just say that some men felt left out!

Research on pregnancy and couples has shown that men have fears, especially with the birth of a first baby, about how the changing circumstances will affect them and their relationship with their partner. Perhaps the important point is how much those concerns are discussed with their partner. In the midst of pregnancy and then birth, a woman's ability to respond to her partner's emotional needs, at a time when she is very needy herself, is a potential problem for men. It may well be that one reason why men do not tend to discuss their own emotional needs at this time is because they recognize the burden their partner will have to bear, and they wish to be seen as manly and supportive. However, research shows that fathers who have anxieties or are depressed are less competent at the fathering role.

Furthermore, an important part of undertaking the fathering role well and confidently is the validation of this fathering role by the man's partner. When a woman is depressed, such validation may be entirely lacking.

With Jane's medical treatment, Paul was excluded from the scene and clearly felt it. The lack of success when it came to a support group for husbands and partners compounded the problem. To some men, there can appear to be a female collusion at play here, which only adds to their feelings of being left out – although, if this happens, it is probably unwittingly. Some interesting Canadian research into PND came up with a surprising finding. It was found that when a man coping with a post-natally depressed wife was provided with support by the health visitor – practical help to do with domestic arrangements, shopping, the kids and so on – it gave the health visitor the opportunity of talking with him. She found that through this avenue, the man opened up to voice his concerns and problems. Pretty good going, considering the man concerned was a Canadian lumberjack type! The amazing result was that when he was given this attention and help, his wife miraculously recovered from her depression. Previously her depression had been intractable – it had not responded to medication or to a female support group.

This has given rise to a full research project looking at whether provision of support services to both the wife and her husband can be a means of helping women recover from being post-natally depressed, and the clinic now runs sessions for depressed mothers and their male partners. Perhaps if a route is found to the man, it allows him to understand his and his partner's predicament and situation, and become a part of the team helping her to recover. In essence, he becomes *part of the solution, not a forgotten part of the problem*. Perhaps all that is needed is for men to go and seek help rather than battling on in isolation, and to have the backing of their partners in getting it for both their benefits. The problem is getting enough men to see that it is in their, and their families', interest to seek that help.

Another aspect of the tales of both male and female partners in this book is the way in which depression caused distress to a couple's relationship.

There are comments from both sides that speak of the extent to which each partner saw their relationship with the other unravelling, in no small measure. Indeed, it is perhaps surprising that more of these relationships did not break up. Perhaps these are the accounts of a group of people who, to a great extent, were the survivors, and there may actually be an unreported group whose relationships did end. At the risk of attempting the impossible, it would seem that some discussion of what depression can do to a relationship is warranted here.

Obviously, relationships and relationship problems are an immense and complex subject, and it would be well beyond me to give a comprehensive or definitive account. Within the research literature, however, the effect of depression in one partner, as it affects the relationship between both partners, has been studied, and there are a few points that might be made with some confidence.

When the word 'depression' is conjured up, perhaps it would not be too far from the truth to say that most people immediately think of aspects such as feeling very low, being unable to cope, being withdrawn and very negative about life. Certainly this happens to a depressed person, but depression also often entails other behaviours as well. Often it is accompanied by increased irritability, hostility and even outright aggression. Once again, the honesty of the personal recollections in this book supports this, as both men and women seem to report experiences of these behaviours, even though they might be put quite diplomatically.

It would not be fair to draw inferences from these personal recollections, and so I shall describe some of the findings from research as they relate to conflict in relationships and to depression. Not everything I say is likely to be well received by all, though, I fear.

Research shows that in a relationship where the female partner is depressed, her levels of hostility and aggression go *up* and, somewhat counterintuitively, it appears that in many cases those of her male partner go *down*.

For the man, the dichotomy between the depressed woman's sadness, inability to cope and helplessness on the one hand, and her hostility, anger and aggressiveness on the other, can be very difficult to respond to in a totally constructive manner. Interestingly, what has been shown is that male partners may provide comfort, sympathy and empathy at the sad times, and they may also try to do the same when their partner is hostile and angry. Unfortunately, this supposedly sends an ambivalent message: it is supportive on the one hand, but not supportive on the other, as sympathy does not validate the depressed female partner's anger and hostility. It has been suggested that this results in a potential to perpetuate her depression. Here is an example of the finding quoted earlier, that the other partner in a relationship with a depressed person is not 'neutral'. To cope with anger and hostility constructively, when it can often be very critical and perhaps hurtful, is very difficult. Alternatively, especially if he is getting depressed also, a male partner can return the hostility and anger out of his own distress. Conflict can then become highly destructive of both individuals and of their relationship.

It would seem to be a situation well worth avoiding, especially when one element of prevention (i.e. emotional support) is not difficult to achieve, and can even be an enjoyable and rewarding part of a relationship.

Interestingly, research on depression in married men has shown that conflict in their relationship is the best single predictor of depression, and unemployment, or the threat of it, and relationship conflict an even more potent cocktail. One of the findings of extensive research conducted in America into marriage and relationships is that women often confront conflict and escalate it, whereas their male partners try to reconcile conflict to a compromise solution and de-escalate it. One of the problems is that in this dynamic, men often then withdraw from the conflict in their relationships, with the result that their partner tends to escalate that conflict even more.

This is sometimes known as a distancer–pursuer or demand–withdrawal pattern of interaction, and it is much more a question of female pursue and demand, and male withdrawal and distance, than vice versa. I certainly felt I could imagine this interactive pattern in some of the accounts. A reality within this dynamic is the uncomfortable fact that the hostility of a man's depressed partner becomes much more than just that, and she is actually physically aggressive towards him.

While it is not necessarily a universally accepted fact, studies of conflict in relationships show that women aggress physically against their male partners as much as, if not more than, their partners do against them. Such a study by this commentator on UK relationships actually showed a higher rate of female-to-male assaults than vice versa, especially for married couples. Five per cent of husbands, as opposed to 1 per cent of wives, reported more than a single category of physical assault against them by their partner.

However, eventually the male may have withdrawn so far he felt that his partner's 'demands' upon him were threatening to overwhelm him.

It doesn't stretch the imagination too far, if this logic is followed, to see that in the end an awfully destructive outcome is highly possible. Of course, in this scenario the male acting out his depression at his situation is then highly likely to be seen by his partner (as I have said before) as him behaving 'badly' rather than 'sadly'.

It would seem to fit the picture that it is women who most frequently seek divorce and separation, and they do so frequently on the grounds of their partner's unreasonable behaviour. The stark reality for men is that a depressed woman may, just in terms of her mental health, be better off ending the relationship, especially if her partner is also depressed.

The Canadian researchers cited earlier run support groups for men experiencing separation and divorce as a part of their community mental health practice. They note that a high percentage of the men coming to them for help are fathers with young babies or children, whose wives or female partners may well have been post-natally depressed. So in the end, post-natal depression in his female partner can have dramatic consequences for a man. He loses his partner, and can lose his child and his home; then he really has got something to be very depressed about. Divorce and separation from a partner or the death of a partner can be the most stressful and disabling of life events. It is no wonder that the rate for separated and divorced men committing suicide is as much as 12–16 times that of others.

A newspaper report of a few years ago illustrates my point all too graphically:

In one tragic case, Michael Mock, who had been sleeping rough after losing his wife, job and home, made a suicide pact with another down and out. He was discovered unconscious after swallowing a cocktail of tranquillisers and rushed to Guy's Hospital. He died after spending four weeks on a ventilator and never regained consciousness. His friend, Leslie Wright, was revived and discharged himself from hospital. He was later found hanged.

In concluding, I note one comment of Cara Aiken's which appeared in an earlier draft of this chapter: 'I think for a while…I even hated the male gender!' Then she added, to her credit: 'That is not the case now.' I hope that the honesty of these personal accounts, together with the details I have added, may be of some assistance to both women and men, and help them to gain a better understanding of the difficulties either partner may face in their relationship where post-natal depression is a factor. Because in the end it is not just the adults that matter – it is the children that matter even more. And they so easily get forgotten.

Post-Natal Illness:
The Professional View

This chapter contains contributions by experts in the field of post-natal illness, together with one by the Association of Post-Natal Illness. The chapter starts with a synopsis by Professor Ian Brockington, explaining the different manifestations of PND.

The psychiatry of childbirth is more complex than any other human situation, because it is a period of rapid biological, social and emotional transition, and exposes the mother to the full gamut of psychological complications, as well as some which result from somatic changes and medical illness. In all, there are at least 20 different psychiatric disorders which occur in the postpartum period (the time after the baby's birth). For simplicity, the main ones may be grouped under five headings:

1. Stress reactions

2. Anxiety disorders

3. Depression

4. Disorders of the mother–infant relationship

5. Puerperal psychosis

This is not a complete list – it omits the *maternity blues* (a transient and trivial disorder), a number of rare psychoses (such as post-eclamptic psychosis), and infanticide (for which there are many causes). But it includes all the main disorders which a midwife should be familiar with.

First, it is important to say something about the normal puerperium (the period from the onset of labour and encompassing the first few weeks of the baby's life).

THE NORMAL PUERPERIUM

For many women, childbirth is a key experience, a supreme moment. It may be followed by excitement, even elation. This may be coupled with exhaustion and physical discomfort. The first few weeks may be a time of severe sleep deprivation. There may be problems and worries over breastfeeding.

There may be difficulty in the mutual adjustment between mother and infant – some infants have a very difficult temperament and do not sleep, or scream inconsolably for hours. Thus, even in normal circumstances, newly delivered mothers are prey to stress, anxieties and emotional upheaval.

1. Stress reactions

These come under the heading of *post-traumatic stress disorder (PTSD)*.

PTSD One should not underestimate the pain and trauma of childbirth for some women, even with the help of modern obstetrics. 'Post-traumatic stress disorder' is a term which refers to the emotional reaction to harrowing experiences. In an effort to assimilate the experience, there is a compulsive need to dwell and ruminate on it, until the horror and shock lose their force. Thus, memories and images intrude into nightmares and waking life for weeks, months or even years. Recently we reported a number of cases from Birmingham (Ballad, Stanley and Brockington 1995). PTSD can have lasting effects, e.g. a phobia for childbirth ('tocophobia').

2. Anxiety disorders

Pregnancy and the puerperium are associated with specific anxiety syndromes. In the puerperium, the most important are puerperal panic, fear of cot death syndrome and phobia for the baby. It is also convenient here to deal with obsessions of child harm.

Puerperal panic is the name given to acute anxiety, experienced particularly by first-time mothers, starting in the maternity hospital or shortly after returning home, when they are confronted with having to care for a fragile and vulnerable newborn. When severe, the picture is not unlike puerperal psychosis, with its early and acute onset, its agitations, incoherence and uncharacteristic behaviour, but it is anxiety about the responsibility for the baby that dominates. There is a grave risk of the baby being taken away– a tragedy, because the disorder is so easily treated. Predisposing social conditions include our isolated nuclear families, living at a distance from family supports. All the difficulties can be avoided if a supportive grandmother or other members of the extended family are at hand.

Fear of cot death syndrome Anxiety about the child is an inescapable aspect of motherhood, but in some mothers it reaches extreme proportions. This is often focused on the remote possibility of sudden infant death. There are mothers who fear to let their infants sleep in case they stop breathing, and those who wake them to see if they are alive. These mothers experience severe insomnia; they may check the infant 20–30 times every night.

Generalized anxiety Even without the specific components of puerperal panic and fear of sudden infant death, the care of an infant, and indeed of young children in general, involves constant vigilance. Some women are, by nature, prone to anxiety and excessive worrying, which can lead to a persistent state of over-arousal. Moll (1920) described 'maternity neurosis', with anxieties about the baby thriving, excessive solicitude and sensitivity to the slightest indication of illness, and the fear that simple tasks would put the baby at risk, e.g. from drowning when being bathed. In some mothers, anxieties about the infant's health resemble an adult Briquet's syndrome – hypochondriacal neurosis-by-proxy.

Phobia for the infant A mother who suffers from excessive anxiety, whatever the cause, may develop a phobic avoidance of her infant, even be unable to approach him at all. This disorder was described by Sved-Williams (1992). In her study, 9 out of 66 mothers admitted to the Adelaide mother and baby unit suffered from phobic infant avoidance, to the degree that staff frequently commented on it. Often the husband was prevented from returning to work.

Author's note

Anxiety disorders Jane is a classic case of severe anxiety disorder. She suffered from puerperal panic, fear of cot death syndrome and phobia for the infant. Her anxiety about her child dying did reach extreme proportions, resulting in 'magical thinking' and obsessiveness. She tried not to bond or make eye contact with her daughter for a while, so that she would 'suffer less if she lost her'. She only had contact with her baby when she really had to.

3. Depression

Although all human beings are prone to depression, it is commonest in women in the reproductive years. Depression is only slightly more common in newly delivered mothers than in other mothers or pregnant women, but it may have serious effects on the developing child and family.

A few women develop recurrent postpartum melancholia. The term 'postpartum (or post-natal) depression' was introduced within the last 40 years, as psychiatrists turned their attention to milder, more common disorders. A major contribution was made by the Gordons in New Jersey (1957–65). They reviewed the literature, studied 100 normal mothers, made a controlled study of aetiological (causal) associations, carried out a follow-through study and showed that social casework was more effective than psychoanalytic treatment (e.g. see

Gordon and Gordon 1957). As a result of a flood of studies in the last 30 years, 'post-natal depression' has become a household term.

Depression after childbirth is clinically similar to any other depression. Its symptoms are those of dysphoric mood, or malaise, in all its variations – sadness, anxiety, irritability or tension; there are self-reproach and pessimism, sometimes with suicidal activity; there are taciturnity and reclusion, loss of vitality, sometimes to the point of self-neglect and role failure; and there are somatic features such as anorexia and insomnia, and impaired mental activity.

Post-natal depression is much more frequent in surveys than in medical consultations. There are, in fact, many more cases of post-natal depression than are actually recorded.

The concept of post-natal depression has the danger of insinuating that there is a homogeneous disorder, which can be investigated and treated as if it had a single cause. Almost all mothers with anxiety, obsessional or post-traumatic disorders, or with a disturbed infant relationship, are depressed, but the setting, the causes and the treatment are different. Nevertheless, it has value as a lay term: it has legitimized maternal depression in the minds of the public, providing a valid explanation for the mothers' distress and role failure, even explaining inexplicable behaviour, such as child neglect and infanticide. It has diminished the stigma of the illness, and enabled mothers to accept that they are ill, and come forward for treatment. It has aroused concern about an important public health problem.

4. Disorders of the mother–infant relationship

Profound disorders of the relationship between mother and baby were first recognized by French forensic physicians, especially Tardieu (1860). The term 'misopaedia' (hatred of children) was introduced by Boileau de Castelnau (1861) and, in Germany, by Oppenheim (1919). Rejection of children has been recognized by child psychiatrists for many years.

The early stages, however, have been neglected. The roots of child rejection are in the early puerperium, even during pregnancy. The symptoms and signs are already evident within days or weeks of the birth. Nevertheless, this important group of disorders, which affect at least 20 per cent of mothers presenting with 'post-natal depression', are poorly recognized by general practitioners, psychiatrists and even specialists in this field. This is the more surprising because these disorders are specific to childbirth. They are in some ways the most specific part of the work of postpartum mental health teams.

Although we can use the term 'mother–infant relationship disorder' as a rubric, there is no single entity; this is a group of overlapping clinical states, with various morbid elements, which include a distressing lack of maternal feeling, anxiety and obsessions, irritability, hostility and aggressive impulses, pathological ideas and outright rejection. These disturbing effects, thoughts and impulses may lead to avoidance, neglect and violent assaults. Clinically they present in a kaleidoscope of combinations. One can recognize four grades of severity – delay in maternal response, hostility, rejection and abuse.

Delay Many mothers are distressed by the absence of the expected feelings for their infants. They do not seem able to feel love like any mother should. They may say that the baby does not seem to be their own – that they are 'baby-sitting'. The reaction of mothers to this state of affairs varies. Some seek reassurance or counsel from their own mothers or confidantes; but some conceal their feelings.

Shame is an important reason why these disorders seldom come to medical attention. Midwives should be aware that this may be a hidden cause of postpartum depression. This is the more important because these states are so easily treated.

Rejection There may be unmistakable rejection – covert or overt. A mother may try to persuade her own mother, or another relative, to take over. She may demand that the infant is fostered or adopted. One of the hallmarks of rejection is feeling dramatically improved when away from the baby. In some mothers the main clinical clue is the attempt to escape. The most poignant manifestation of rejection is the secret wish that the baby 'disappear' – be stolen, or die. Some mothers have the courage, or the desperation, to make these wishes explicit.

Hostility Rejecting mothers often feel tense and angry in the presence of the infant, and may make vicious remarks. Anger with the child is often expressed first by shouting at it. Very common is an urge to shake a crying baby, initially gripping it tightly and shaking it lightly a few times, but in more serious incidents, shaking it violently. The mother may have impulses to strangle or suffocate the child. She may feel the urge to throw it on the floor, against the wall or over the balcony; as a precursor of more serious assaults, she may handle it roughly, or throw it into the cot.

Abuse Savage aggression, cruelty and neglect take an extraordinary variety of forms – shaking, beating, wrenching the limbs, bites, burns, asphyxiation, poisoning, starvation and sequestration. The term 'Munchausen-by-proxy' is applied to the condition of mothers who pretend their child is ill, or deliberately induce illness in order to get medical attention. Severe child abuse occurs in 3–6 out of 1000 infants. Death due to abuse is the fate of about one in ten thousand infants; in most of such cases, the intemperate parent is motivated to punish the child, rather than kill it. Neglecting mothers have a profound impairment of 'bonding'.

Author's note

Disorders of the mother–infant relationship: Delay Rosemary, Julie, Pippa, Laura, Gail, Jenny, Sarah, Veritee and myself all suffered from delayed feelings of love for our children. Professor Brockington hits the nail on the head when he describes a feeling of 'baby-sitting'. We have each commented on the fact that the child did not feel like our own – it could have been anyone's, we were just looking after it.

Rejection I experienced outright rejection towards Georgina, my first child. I didn't want her, I felt I had made a grave mistake – I even wanted her to die. I asked my mother to take her away. I did have the courage to express my wish – I *was* desperate.

Hostility I often felt tense and angry around my children. Their crying made me violent – not towards the children but towards objects and myself. It was sheer frustration. Pippa and Veritee admit to feeling 'harmful' towards their babies at a particular stage, but they never acted on their feelings – I feel sure that their reaction was pure frustration too.

5. Puerperal psychosis

This is a very serious illness that affects one to three mothers in a thousand. It is an acute psychosis developing within the first few weeks (usually the first ten days) after delivery, and having a clinical picture of mania, depressive psychosis or 'atypical psychosis'.

Those with mania are excited, loquacious, disinhibited and intensely overactive. Those with depression differ from mothers suffering from 'post-natal depression' in the great severity of their condition and the presence of features like confusion, delusions and stupor. The atypical psychoses (sometimes called 'cycloid psychoses') have confusion or perplexity, catatonic features, thought disorder, auditory hallucinations and delusions. The onset is acute and treatment requires admission to a psychiatric hospital where either ECT or a combination of drugs is used to treat the disorder.

Author's note

Puerperal psychosis Laura is the only person in this book who actually suffered from this severe form of post-natal illness. This disorder is extreme, and I hope that her account will give you an accurate insight into the illness from someone who has used her experience positively in helping other women overcome their depression.

Ann Herreboudt, midwife counsellor, St John and St Elizabeth Hospital, St John's Wood, London, writes:

I work as a midwife counsellor with Yehudi Gordon [an expert obstetrician on natural childbirth], with whom I have worked for the last 12 years. My main role in the obstetric unit is that of ante-natal and post-natal support person. This includes one-to-one sessions, family sessions and family group sessions, and my main interest is in the development of the family.

THE SADNESS OF POST-NATAL DEPRESSION

The saddest part of PND, for those whose condition is not detected early, is that, when recognized, it can be greatly helped. Talk therapy is proved to be one of the best approaches. It seems that because the woman concerned cannot say, 'I have post-natal depression', no one makes the diagnosis. The diagnosis seems to be made with hindsight.

The second level of sadness is the inability of pregnant women to peer beyond their labour, so we have to be very careful how we talk to them in pregnancy and give them some insight into the reality of living with a baby. There also seems to be a secretiveness amongst parents, especially those with young babies, which feeds into the impression that we are given that all young babies are very manageable, when the reality is exactly the opposite.

We still feel that the baby will fit in with us. The truth is that we have to fit in with the baby, but getting that across to pregnant couples can be very, very difficult.

THE INTERNAL CHILD

It is perfectly true to say that within ourselves there is an internal child which, for a lot of pregnant couples, becomes quite real. It is very common for a pregnant woman to sense or fear, or try to avoid, feelings related to those she had as a child herself, and the same is true of the father: memories, and a recognition of how he may have felt, can come to the forefront again. This tends to occur at a time when the parents of the pregnant couple may wish to dominate them, to relive pregnancy and birth themselves, then bring the baby up in the same way that they themselves brought up theirs. Part of this is a desire to keep things the same as when *they* were young parents, and it may be that, subconsciously, they are avoiding the fact that perhaps they got it slightly wrong, or that it was not quite right for their particular child.

ANTE-NATAL DETECTION

The rate of ante-natal pick-up of suspected or possible post-natal depression can be very high, but the questions asked need to specifically focus on the emotional state of the parents-to-be (and I do mean both parents). For instance, with the normal ante-natal booking, obstetric and surgical history will be taken, but certain key questions may not be asked, such as:

'Did your mother have post-natal depression?'

'Have you ever been depressed or treated for depression?'

'Do you remember your childhood?' (Bad memories may need to be looked at.)

'What are your expectations of the birth, the baby and becoming a family?' (If the expectations are unrealistic or 'true romantic', then the chances of feeling let down are very high.)

Partners need to be asked these same questions.

Some other questions which need to be asked and which are important in the detection of depression, ante-natally and post-natally, are linked to the mother's nutritional habits and diet. For example:

'What is your diet like?'

'Has there been anorexia in the family/have you suffered from anorexia?'

'Does your weight go up and down?'

'How do you feel about your weight gain and body in pregnancy?'

The emotional aspect of these questions is more important than the physical. A very much altered body is acceptable to most women, but some find it very difficult to cope with.

Irrational expectations of life with a new baby can lead to disappointment. No baby sleeps all night and feeds just twice a day, but again, because of the climate of secrecy out there, the media image gives the impression that it is 'the good parent' that has the baby that sleeps all night. Therefore, this type of question should also be asked:

'How do you feel about the baby?'

'How do you feel the baby may behave?'

If any potential problems in these areas are picked up, then looking at them ante-natally can lead to a lot of improvement, even repair in some cases.

POST-NATAL GRIEF

For some mothers, there are feelings of grief at the end of pregnancy and child-birth, when the mother grieves the loss of the pregnancy, the loss of the child inside her, and sometimes finds it difficult to relate to the baby in her arms because she so much wants a baby back inside her.

The other cause for grief can be the loss of one's old self, the old self that one knew and recognized so well. Suddenly you're a mum, suddenly you have the responsibility of a baby, your body has changed, you don't go out to work, you don't wear high-heeled shoes, and a lot of women do find this transition quite difficult. They suffer all the signs of grief – not necessarily post-natal depression, but anger, confusion, restlessness, general feelings of unhappiness. The relationship between husband and wife also changes. The concentration goes to the baby and both partners can feel jealous of the baby and rejected by the other. For men, having to go back to work and get on as though life hasn't changed can be very difficult. In fact life has changed very much, and what goes on at home most men do not really talk about, for there is very little help and support for them out there.

Author's note

The sadness of post-natal depression As Ann Herreboudt says, one of the problems is 'the inability of pregnant women to peer beyond their labour'. There is a definite secretiveness amongst parents – I discuss this 'myth of perfect mothering' in Chapter 15 quite comprehensively.

The internal child I have covered this aspect, too, in Chapter 15, under 'Our own parents' influence' and 'Effects from our own childhood'. I strongly believe that our childhoods and our childhood memories can contribute to depression after childbirth. Six of us out of the ten case studies reveal a link with childhood.

Antenatal detection I like Ann Herreboudt's ideas for ante-natal pick-up of suspected or possible post-natal depression. If all ante-natal teams were to take this suggestion on board, I think that many new mothers displaying signs of possible depression could be watched more closely and given increased support from their local clinic during the first few post-natal months. This would perhaps not prevent PND, but it could lead to early detection and early treatment.

Post-natal grief From the ten personal accounts in this book, I have noticed that one common link is the fact that we were all confident, outgoing and independent women. Eight of us enjoyed our careers – which may, in contrast to looking after a new-born baby, have seemed very exciting on reflection. The adaptation from being carefree and independent, perhaps even slightly irresponsible, is very difficult indeed – the loss of one's old self. I do believe this theory to be quite accurate, and a definite contribution to the onset of depression.

It is also very difficult for some of us to adapt to the changes in our body shape during and after pregnancy. Our image changes and we have all expressed the sadness of a poor self-image. Feelings of resentment can manifest, especially as our partners appear 'untouched' by fatherhood, in comparison.

Three health visitors working for the East Hertfordshire NHS Trust write:

We have 20, 13 and 10 years' experience respectively, and are giving this information from our specific area in Hertfordshire. Other geographical areas will probably be different, with different services available.

AWARENESS AND METHODS OF DETECTING POST-NATAL DEPRESSION, AND THE SUPPORT OFFERED

In our experience, there has been increased awareness in recent years about PND amongst all health professionals, but particularly health visitors. We feel that it is extremely important to increase that awareness in all parents with young families, and ante-natal mothers.

In our area, health visitors take part in ante-natal classes run for parents in the evening. The 'baby blues' and post-natal depression are discussed, so that both new parents are made aware of the symptoms. And it is stressed that, if these feelings do not go away, it is important to seek advice from the health visitor or GP. Male partners are encouraged to be aware of how their wives are feeling.

It is essential to give this information ante-natally, as first-time mothers, particularly, will have no experience of child-rearing or about how they are likely to feel after the birth. They may not know what is 'normal', so they may be unable to recognize the symptoms of post-natal depression. In our area, PND is also discussed at mother and baby groups run by the health visitors. The NCT (National Childbirth Trust) discusses it too.

It is essential that health visitors encourage pregnant women to attend ante-natal classes from whatever source.

In our area, training in the detection of post-natal depression is currently underway for all health visitors across the Trust. We shall be studying the use of *the Edinburgh PND Scale* (a two-day course), which is to be used with mothers at six weeks, four months and eight months post-natally. There is an awareness of the importance of training all health visitors in using this technique.

We all work in close liaison with the GPs. Depressed mothers are always referred to their GP.

There is a support group run jointly by a health visitor and a community psychiatric nurse, where a crèche is available. The philosophy of our support group is to facilitate peer-group support: here, a post-natally depressed mother is able to talk to other mothers with the same condition, in an informal environment.

The aims of our group are: to provide an environment conducive to peer-group support; to provide an initial block of ten Edinburgh PND Scale sessions for each referred post-natally depressed mother (the situation can be reviewed at the end of this time and further sessions are offered if thought to be beneficial); to provide a crèche – one hour in the week when a mother has time for herself; to encourage the formation of smaller peer-led groups, to follow on from these sessions; to provide any relevant advice and/or health education requested by group members; to increase group members' confidence and self-esteem.

We provide two facilitators (helpers) at each group session. We offer: a flexible programme of health education dealing with topics such as PND, stress- and anger-management, relaxation, self-awareness, how to cope with a crying baby; support – the group supports the individual and the individual supports others; confidentiality – mothers can talk within the group in a safe setting. Ground rules will be set and agreed by the whole group.

To evaluate individual effectiveness, the Edinburgh Post-Natal Depression Scale (EPDS) will be used on all new members of the group and repeated at the end of the ten sessions. If further sessions are warranted, the EPDS will be repeated every three weeks thereafter. To evaluate the effectiveness of the group, we will monitor the individual EPDS scores, client and group leader performances, attendance figures, and verbal feedback. We will refer women to the appropriate agencies and liaise with them, if a problem is identified.

Leaflets on 'baby blues' and post-natal depression are given to mothers during home visits to the new baby. Leaflets are also available at the health centre and doctor's surgery.

We hope that there is a growing awareness of PND amongst the general public.

Author's note

It is refreshing to see a local NHS Trust offering such an excellent service. Not all are alike. This group of health visitors very obviously do understand and recognize the need for increased awareness in all parents with young families, and ante-natal mothers.

The support group is an excellent idea, giving mothers the opportunity to air their feelings informally but within a 'safe' environment, and attended also by the health visitor and community psychiatric nurse. Talking is a major healer – but mothers need to be strongly encouraged to do so, to feel safe and unthreatened and to be able to trust someone wholeheartedly, before they will talk.

Pauline Maddinson, liaison health visitor, Queen Elizabeth II Hospital, Welwyn Garden City, East Hertfordshire NHS Trust, writes:

THE ROLE OF THE LIAISON HEALTH VISITOR WITH THE MOTHER
AND BABY UNIT

The role of the liaison health visitor with the mother and baby unit has developed as the unit has expanded from two to six beds, as the understanding of the extent and effects of post-natal illness in the mother, baby and father has increased, and as the detection of PND in the community has improved.

Visits are made daily to the unit in response to any concerns that staff may have about the health of the babies and their development, and to discuss with mothers any queries or anxieties that they may have regarding their babies – for example, about immunizations, weaning, etc. Links have been established with the paediatric assessment unit (for babies that are unwell) and with the children's out-patients department for on-going problems, immunization and developmental checks; and it is possible to discuss concerns with senior nurses and doctors. The health promotions resources department is regularly contacted for leaflets on all topics, which are then displayed on the unit.

The liaison health visitor's role includes regular attendance at, and active participation in, ward meetings and care programme approach meetings together with other members of the multidisciplinary team (consultant, doctor, senior nurse, occupational therapist and liaison social worker). She maintains regular communication with the family health visitor, and if the family live locally she is encouraged to maintain contact with them while the mother is on the ward. Particularly valuable are home visits made when the mother is on leave from the unit, and the liaison health visitor is able to supply them with feedback.

The ward is usually full and busy, and when appropriate, a post-natal support group is initiated (very similar to groups that are set up in the community). There are three to four sessions, lasting about an hour, covering such topics as the experience of pregnancy and childbirth; how the women feel about themselves as mothers; their hopes and expectations; balancing babies' needs and parents' needs; and an introduction to the importance of touch and massage.

The consultant-led unit is very aware of the effects of post-natal illness on the whole family. A meeting once a month has been initiated for fathers/partners, to create an opportunity to discuss some of their concerns and needs. And a support group for both parents, part social and part informative, meets, as the need arises, for several sessions.

Topics that have been discussed include:

- understanding medication and post-natal illness
- the importance of play
- resuscitation
- aromatherapy, with contributions on the subject from parents
- swimming safety, toy safety.

Other aspects of the liaison health visitor's role involve liaison with the children's ward and special-care maternity department and with health visitors in the community. This is very much a two-way process, and occasionally I am asked to see mothers if staff are concerned about them. The knowledge and understanding acquired while working with the mother and baby unit have proved quite valuable on several occasions.

With so few units, and so few beds in the county, it is a real privilege to be a member of a multidisciplinary team, doing such important work with families at such an early stage.

Dr Tessa Dormon MB, BS, general practitioner, Hoddesdon, Hertfordshire, writes:

Post-natal depression

As a general practitioner and a member of the primary healthcare team, caring for women through their pregnancies and post-delivery is usually a positive and rewarding experience. Prior knowledge of the woman enables one to be more aware of behavioural changes which may signify post-natal depression. Members of the primary healthcare team are ideally placed to look for depression, as they will be seeing the mother and baby at frequent intervals in the first few weeks post-delivery.

Women may present themselves with feelings of anxiety and hopelessness, although they will often have 'soldiered on' for weeks, sometimes months, because of feeling ashamed and guilty that they are unable to cope. Relatives such as husbands or parents may express their concern, in which case an opportunity needs to be made to review the woman concerned.

Within our practice, treatment is by counselling, giving the woman a chance to voice her problems and concerns, and/or by using medication. Input from all members of the team is vital, and regular communication is of great importance.

Much of what follows is based on my personal experience as a general practitioner over the last fifteen years.

INCIDENCE

Depression is a very common illness presenting to the primary care team, and is more common in women than men. It has a peak incidence between the ages of 25 and 45 (Leopold Zoscchnick, *The Female Patient,* 1997). Post-natal depression can affect anything between 3 and 20 per cent of women after childbirth. Figures of 26 to 32 per cent have been quoted of adolescents who develop PND. Rates of recurrence in subsequent pregnancies vary between 10 and 35 per cent. There is an increased risk of PND if the woman has a previous history of depression. The illness needs to be distinguished from the 'baby blues', which can affect up to 70 per cent of women post-delivery, and the much rarer post-puerperal psychosis, which affects 0.1 to 0.2 per cent of women post-delivery. Post-natal depression is more common than pre-eclampsia, toxaemia, gestational diabetes and pre-term deliveries, but, sadly, is often missed by healthcare professionals.

PRESENTATION

The baby blues are characterized by emotional ups and downs (lability), feelings of vulnerability, crying and poor sleep, usually starting within one week of birth. Post-puerperal psychosis is comparatively rare, with psychiatric features including mood change, excitable mood (hypomania), mania, hallucinations and feelings of hopelessness.

Post-natal depression presents with a wide variety of symptoms, including panic attacks, lack of joy (anhedonia), inappropriate mood (dysphoric mood), a slowing down of mind and body (psychomotor retardation), changes in appetite and sleep, and feelings of inadequacy and guilt – particularly, failure at motherhood. There may be excessive anxiety over the baby's health. Physical symptoms include headaches, chest pains, palpitations, hyperventilation and tingling of the limbs. PND usually presents within the first six weeks after the baby's birth, and 60 per cent of women will have symptoms before six months. It may be far longer before it is recognized, and it can range from mild to severe.

DETECTION

Members of the primary healthcare team are in an ideal position to look for post-natal depression. Community midwives and health visitors will have contact with the mother and newborn in the early days and, depending on local practice, the GP will see mother and child at least once within the first week. The six-week check of the baby and the mother's post-natal check provide an ideal opportunity for inquiring about symptoms of depression. Questions may need to be specifically tailored to the situation, in that, for example, nearly all mothers of newborns will suffer from disturbed sleep, and early-morning waking may call for specific inquiry. Suicidal intent needs to be looked for – inquiring about it does not increase the risk of suicide. The Edinburgh PND Scale (see pages 127–128) is a useful tool to administer if post-natal depression is suspected.

AETIOLOGY

The aetiology (cause) of post-natal depression is complex and is probably multifactorial (i.e. there are a lot of possible factors). The levels of the hormone oestrogen rise to ten times the normal levels during pregnancy, and return to pre-pregnant levels within three days of delivery. Likewise, progesterone levels drop precipitously after delivery. *Prolactin* (a hormone produced by the pituitary gland that is important during breast feeding) levels drop far more slowly. It has been suggested that the changes of hormone levels are related to the development of post-natal depression. Mode of delivery has been cited as affecting the likelihood of developing it.

Women who have emergency Caesarean sections are more likely to develop PND than those who have instrumental vaginal deliveries, who in their turn are more likely to be affected than those who have normal vaginal deliveries. Likewise, mothers who deliver pre-term infants are at an increased risk.

TREATMENT

Post-natal depression appears to respond well to standard anti-depressant drugs. Of prime importance is whether or not the mother is breastfeeding. If she is, it is advisable to use a tricyclic anti-depressant such as Dothiepin or Amitiptyline. These drugs are not found in quantifiable amounts in breast milk. The tricyclic anti-depressants have a large number of side-effects, and are toxic in overdose, which is important if there is a high suicide risk. If the mother is not breastfeeding, an SSRI (selective serotonin reuptake inhibitor) such as fluoxetine (Prozac) can be used. The SSRIs have far fewer side-effects, and are safer in overdose. Whichever drug is used, support from the family and health professionals involved is necessary, and formal follow-up and evaluation of the treatment must be carried out on a regular basis. Drug treatment can be combined with psychotherapy, which is useful for those with more severe symptoms. If there is a very high suicide risk, patients may require admission to a mother and baby unit, and in recalcitrant cases ECT has been used with good effect.

There has been much discussion of the use of oestrogen patches in the management of post-natal depression, and a large study carried out showed a significant, rapid, stable fall in both patient- and doctor-rated depression scores of the oestrogen-treated group as compared to those who had taken placebos. Post-natal depression support groups can also provide valuable information and counselling.

PREVENTION

Awareness of post-natal depression is very important, as all the contributors to this book have pointed out. Pregnant women need screening for risk factors such as a past history of either depression or post-natal depression. It has been shown that women at risk may benefit from pre-natal *psychosocial interventions* (a form of professional social support) – for example, education about parenthood, about the need to have help when the baby arrives, and about prioritizing the demands of family, house, baby and self.

CONCLUSION

Post-natal depression is a devastating illness at a time which should be happy and fulfilling for the woman and her family. With the education of both healthcare professionals and pregnant women, it can be detected and treated effectively in the majority of women at an early stage.

Clare Delpech, for the Association of Post-Natal Illness, writes:

This book, which has been caringly crafted by Cara Aiken, uses women's own stories, including her own, to illustrate how it feels to experience post-natal mental illness.

Cara does not seek to shock or torment us; she has not sought out extreme cases of this type of illness. Nevertheless, the raw suffering and pain of these women's stories leave the reader with a lasting impression. Cara has chosen women with different lifestyles, and this will help readers to identify with them more closely, and understand more easily why a depressive illness just after childbirth can be so disabling both to the sufferer and to her immediate family.

Cara does more than just tell us 'how it feels' to have PND. She has positive suggestions about how women can cope if they suffer from this illness. The women in her book also speak out, with strongly felt opinions, about their illness and treatment.

It is very rare that a book containing such painful experiences of depression can be recommended to current sufferers, but this book is an exception. It seeks to illuminate rather than to alarm; it offers hope rather than reinforcing despair. Few sufferers can dare to believe, when they are in the depths of their illness, that one day they will stumble out of the darkness and emerge into the light again. Cara takes us on this journey with her companions and lets them speak about their feelings and conclusions as they try to make sense of the illness that has affected them.

Importantly, this is a book of hope. Sufferers who read it will recognize that these women really have 'been there' but that they have all recovered and are healthy people again. I recommend this book to those who want an insight into the feelings that accompany an episode of post-natal illness, whether they are fellow-sufferers, the families of sufferers, health professionals or interested lay people.

The Association for Post-Natal Illness was set up in 1979 in order

- to provide support to mothers suffering from post-natal illness
- to increase public awareness of the illness
- to encourage research into its cause and nature.

The work of the Association is essential, as post-natal illness affects between 70,000 and 100,000 women and their babies in this country every year. It is rightly called 'the silent epidemic':

Sadly, despite greater tolerance of mental illness and sympathetic press coverage on the subject, three-quarters of those women who suffer from post-natal depression will not seek any form of medical help. *They suffer alone and unaided and often for prolonged periods of time.* (Dr Vivette Glover)

Post-natal depression is the main cause of maternal suicide after childbirth in the UK. (Professor Brice Pitt)

Post-natal depression causes measurable cognitive problems for the children of depressed mothers ... If the illness is diagnosed early, *treatment reduces the suffering* and the damaging effects of the illness on the family, *especially the child.* (Dr Lyn Murray)

SUPPORT

The Association has over seven hundred volunteers throughout the country who have recovered from post-natal illness. These women support others who are currently ill on a one-to-one basis. This offers proof to sufferers that they can, and *will*, get better. The volunteers are backed up by the Association's trained staff and medical experts, who can be called upon to give advice when necessary.

SAFEGUARDS

The relationship between the Association and the medical profession is close and harmonious. Our committee ensures that, as far as possible, women who approach the organization are safeguarded from some of the possible disadvantages of being counselled by untrained volunteers.

All support relationships are regularly monitored. Supporters and sufferers can contact our staff at any time if the relationship is causing concern to either. Women who approach the Association do so knowing that any information given to the organization is treated in the strictest confidence. Information is never released to outside bodies, other organizations or the media.

TREATMENT

Effective treatment for post-natal illness is available. The Association is promoting the use of the Edinburgh PND Scale (see p.127–128) to encourage early detection, so that it can be traced before it becomes so severe and disabling that hospital treatment may be needed. By shortening the time a mother is ill, the effect on the child is considerably reduced.

SPECIALIST CLINIC

The Association supports the only specialist post-natal illness out-patient clinic in the country. This is a place where seeking psychiatric help is far more acceptable to sufferers. It is hoped that the success of the clinic will encourage other health authorities to fund similar projects to facilitate the treatment of women who would otherwise suffer unaided.

PUBLICATIONS

Post-natal Depression, published by the Association, is designed to help mothers suffering from post-natal illness to help themselves. It describes symptoms, medical treatment and self-help strategies. *The Baby Blues and Post-natal Depression* is an informative leaflet distributed to maternity units and ante-natal clinics. This publication is designed to make women more aware of the illness, so that medical advice can be sought at an early stage by those who are affected.

At the moment, there is a huge demand for this leaflet. As we are unable to meet these demands for free, only some of the health authorities (those of have the funding and those who choose to use their funds in this way) order the publications. However, if new mothers request leaflets personally, then the Association will send information packs to them free of charge.

14

Practical Advice and Conclusions

Each individual who figures in this book has her own opinion as to why she personally suffered from post-natal depression. In each case, the symptoms of the illness were all very similar. Some of the many common factors linked with the cause of PND for all the contributors were: partner's lack of emotional support and understanding; general lack of practical support; isolation (living in a rural place, recently having moved home); stress factors including those associated with house move, marriage problems, financial worries, physical illness, family health etc.; unwanted interference; own experience of childhood and/or relation-ship with own parents; lack of knowledge on how to deal with a baby; lack of information about PND prior to having a baby (absence of ante-natal discussions on the subject); the feeling that PND is a taboo subject which inhibits discussion – hence late diagnosis and treatment; vulnerability due to low emotional state; the impact of society's attitude and of the media image – having a baby = ultimate joy and fulfilment ('so what's wrong with me?'); traumatic birth experience; difficult pregnancy; feeling of having to continue being 'indispensable', a pillar of strength to family and friends – not wanting to let anyone down, even though feeling unable to cope; ethnic origin – family's expectations as to mother's role; hormone imbalance.

What is so important is how each person feels she *should* have been treated. Having had the first-hand experience of post-natal illness, each has gained some very strong ideas. With this in mind, I asked everyone who has given an account of her experience here to write her conclusion, as this book would not exist without these women's contributions. They deserve the opportunity to express their opinions publicly.

I hope that their suggestions and advice on coping with PND will help other women in the future – these people have all been brave enough to speak up and to state how *they* think the illness should be dealt with.

Cara

As mothers, we have our own ideals about what we should be doing with our children and how we should be bringing them up. The mechanics of dealing with them present little problem. Anyone can feed, clean or change a child, even if on autopilot. But what we expect of ourselves at the level of stimulation is quite different. Some of us just simply do not enjoy entertaining a very young child. There is little reward in the early stages, and for feeling that way, we in turn feel *guilty* – the biggest word, in my opinion, linked with motherhood.

I do not feel that it is wrong to need or want time apart from the children, to spend an evening or weekend alone with your partner, to go out with friends for the day or just do nothing but be 'you' for a while. If we are feeling depressed, irritable and miserable, surely it can only benefit the child to be with other carers for certain periods? It is not much fun for the mother or for the child to be in the same unhappy atmosphere constantly, both feeling entrapped by the situation.

I feel that it was a very important decision for me to return to work, if only on a part-time basis. Although I was still suffering from post-natal depression at this time, the hours away from my 'real life' helped me on to the road of recovery and gave me back some much needed independence and mental stimulation. I was lucky to have my dear friend Val offer to look after my two children, in my own home, which enabled me to leave their routine totally undisturbed with the added comfort of knowing that they were in the hands of someone they loved dearly. I could leave my home in the mornings, completely guilt-free. Returning to work did me the world of good and I feel sure, with hindsight, that this eventually ended my depression.

It is very important to remember that no one ever compiled a list of rules on what we should achieve with our children. Whatever we as individuals are able to give, *willingly* and *happily*, to our children is acceptable.

CARA'S SELF-HELP HINTS AND TIPS

1. Rest – make sure you get enough rest, and take every opportunity to sleep.
2. Learn some relaxation techniques.
3. Eat well and at regular intervals.
4. Ask for help.
5. Do not be afraid to admit that you are not coping.
6. Avoid excessive amounts of intoxicants, e.g. alcohol, caffeine.
7. Write down your feelings.
8. If you are feeling angry or violent and these feelings are frightening you, share them with someone you can trust.

Rosemary

'My children are now 15 and 16 years old. I enjoy their company immensely and I think they are wonderful. However, when I was asked to write about my first years as a mother, my initial reaction was sheer horror at the thought of having to relive them in my mind. I suppose I can best describe the comparative stress of them as follows: I am a successful professional with many publications, undertake frequent business trips to different parts of the world where I negotiate with government personnel who are at the top of their profession and I am praised for the huge amount of work that I regularly do under constant pressure. However, all the pressures and stress of work pale into insignificance when compared with the stress and difficulty of being a mother of babies and young children. There is simply no comparison, and I laugh with derision when I read articles describing the troubles of businessmen.

'A very important change for me was going back to work and hiring a professionally trained nanny and someone to clean the house twice a week. I realize that these last two options are not open to everyone, but reaffirming my identity as a professional and regularly getting away from the domestic atmosphere and chores were what enabled me to recover from my depression. I also began to recover my husband's respect, for he recognized the value of my professional work. In my experience, going to the office is having a rest compared with the life of a housewife with young children.

'Perhaps the story of my experience makes me sound as though I was an uncaring mother. I don't think so – it is rather that caring mothers are portrayed as earth mother types, baking bread and cakes and adoring the domestic life. Some are like that and I am happy for them, but I do not believe that is necessary in order to be an adequate mother. After all, most mothers who stay at home are doing housework for most of the day and not spending it with their children at all. My view is that all children need is to feel that they are loved and that they are important.

'As both my children have turned out fine, are doing well at school and are responsible, caring teenagers, obviously what I did was good enough, despite all the criticism I received. When I look back to what I did with them, it amounted to the following: lots of hugs and kisses, praise when they did something right, and I read them a lot of stories and looked at books with them. All other childhood pastimes – toys, Lego, etc. – I found cripplingly boring and therefore did not involve myself with them. However, I was able to do what I did do much better once I returned to work – I appreciated the children much more after having been out most of the day than when I was at home all the time.

'Yes, I did have some guilt-creating scenes – namely, the children crying when I left for work and begging me not to go, but I can assure you that those scenes had no lasting effect on them. The nanny said that the second I left, they were back to normal. Another important improvement was taking time with my husband alone – i.e. going out some evenings and taking holidays with each other alone, which we did for the first time when my daughter was three. We should have done it before.

'I am convinced that it is most important to keep oneself reasonably happy, for children sense a parent's unhappiness and become grouchy themselves, thus creating a vicious circle.'

Jane

'I feel that midwives, health visitors and GPs should be much more aware of the possibility of PND and more willing to treat it or refer women on to specialist mother and baby units. Mothers should be encouraged to make use of parent and toddler groups, as isolation can play a large part in PND. It was several months before it was suggested to me that I attended any groups – new mums don't always realize (I certainly didn't) that you don't actually have to have a toddler to go to most toddler groups.

'I know that, for me, starting to attend such groups wasn't a cure, but it did make getting through the day a little easier. Groups such as the National Childbirth Trust should be much more up-front about their existence and what they have to offer. When I eventually started attending local parent and toddler groups, I met someone who was involved with the NCT and went along to an open house that she told me about. Although I had heard of the NCT, at the time when I needed the kind of support it can offer it was purely by chance that I found out about our local branch's activities.

'Women and their partners must not allow themselves to be fobbed off by health professionals. If they feel that all is not well, they owe it to themselves and their baby to get support. Midwives should be more alert to the possibility of a woman becoming post-natally depressed. After the birth of my first child, I was extremely anxious. On the occasions that I mentioned this, the midwife was quite dismissive. Consequently, I felt unable to discuss my fears in any depth with her. Also, I still feel bitter that it took five months for my PND to be diagnosed and seven months before I was seen by a psychiatrist. The health visitor was seeing me regularly throughout this time, yet didn't pick up on any of my concerns. In fact, her apparent inability to see how ill I really was added to my confusion, as I knew that something must be wrong for me to feel so awful.

'Even now I feel that had I been diagnosed earlier, I might not have suffered so badly or for so long.

'I was fortunate that when my illness was finally diagnosed, I had access to perhaps the best mother and baby unit available. We should all be campaigning to make sure that these kinds of facilities are available to all families who need them.

'There needs to be much greater discussion and recognition of post-natal depression so that it is no longer a taboo subject. Ex-sufferers should try to be open about their experiences so that more people are aware of how common and how devastating it is. It would also have been of enormous help to my partner and me if his workmates had been more sympathetic. When I was at my most ill, I was unable to be left alone with the children. Paul had to miss a lot of work but, far from being supported by his colleagues, he met with a lot of hostility. I think this is a question of ignorance and prejudice about mental illness in general, as I assume attitudes would have been different had I been debilitated through physical illness.

'I think we all have false expectations of parenthood. The view we are fed via the media is very different from the reality of life with a baby. For a long time I pretended to everyone that I was coping. Only my partner, Paul, was aware that things really weren't OK, but even he didn't know the true extent of my problem. I was, and still am if I'm honest, envious of friends who appeared to be coping, although I realize that sometimes they probably weren't coping all that well either.

'I think some of the issues surrounding PND are ones of identity. For instance, when I was ill, I thought I should feel how I felt prior to having children. I now realize that motherhood changes your outlook, values and aspirations for ever. Now I don't expect to be as I was – my priorities and interests have changed, but I enjoy my new life.

'Daisy is now at school, Jacob attends playgroup three mornings a week and I take him to parent and toddler groups. I host a National Childbirth Trust open house, am training to be a breastfeeding counsellor, and am involved in an award scheme which encourages venues in Birmingham to support breastfeeding. I also do voluntary telephone supporting for the Association of Post-Natal Illness, and I'm a trustee of a new mental health charity.

'I realize that when both children are in school full-time, we will have a better standard of living if I return to work, but for now I am happy to be a stay-at-home mother and involve myself in voluntary work.

'My advice for mothers who think they are suffering from PND is to get a diagnosis as soon as possible if you suspect that all is not well. Get professional help. Attend mother and toddler groups (even with a new-born baby) to avoid being isolated. Talk about it – don't be ashamed, and don't try to cover up how bad you are feeling.

'Do not try to live up to false expectations or compare yourself to mothers who are coping.'

Julie

'Well, life will never be the same! If I'd known then what I know now, would I still have become a mum? YES! Children do zap most of your energy, but they charge you back up with a great boost too. Of course, I wish I'd known more about childcare – books do have an index, but I couldn't find "how to be a good mum" anywhere! I do wish that I hadn't had PND, that I'd known more about it, how to spot it and deal with it. I just didn't enjoy my little baby as I should have done, and I do still regret that. Michael suffered, too, by acquiring a Jekyll and Hyde wife, and he still doesn't know what happened to the woman he married.

'The main problem I had was *me*. If my hormones hadn't decided to do a jig I'd have felt a damn sight better, then and now. However, even with the ups and downs, I don't regret having Sarah for a minute. It's nice to be called "mum" and have my daughter and family. It does take time to adjust to your life not being your own any more. I don't have much time for *me* and *us*. A lie-in together as a couple is a rare treat, but we do enjoy the family cuddles and breakfast in bed, sticky fingers and crumbs and all. OK, having a baby has turned my life upside down, and me inside out, but I wouldn't swop it for all the tea in China.

'There was never any talk about my not returning to work – like a lot of mums, I had to. I've often felt too tired after a stressful day at work to really take notice of Sarah, and have instead watched the clock, waiting for her bedtime and "peace". I still feel a little resentful that I never had the choice to stay at home, at least part-time, but I do spend quality time with Sarah now, which is much better than my constantly screaming at her all day because I've no patience. My weekends have become a mixture of heaven and hell. Working all week means that household chores take place during the weekend when I would really like to spend the time with my daughter and husband.

'To all working mums, I would like to say: Don't feel guilty when the persecutors come out in force. You're doing what you think is best for your family. If you're a better person having some release, some freedom and independence, then you're going to be a better mum, and that's what counts!

'Unfortunately, my depression is still present, and Sarah is now two and a half years old. The old symptoms of tiredness, inability to sleep, comfort eating, loss of libido, irritability, weepiness etc. have returned. I've had two changes of anti-depressants, with another looming, as the current ones are stimulating my brain chemicals so much, I just can't sleep. I am tired of still feeling like this, but after hearing about other mothers who took a while to recover fully, I don't feel as abnormal as I did, and I know *it will get better*. My doctor has now referred me to a psychiatrist, a decision I am very nervous about, but maybe as well as chemical and hormonal changes in my body, past childhood problems may be aggravating my condition.

'If it can put me back to how I was, then I'll just have to swallow my pride, and ignore the stigma. *I want to be well. I will be well.* It just might take a little longer than I expected. I have obsessive thoughts that my GP is sick of the sight of me but he is the only person who can, hopefully, sort me out. I cut down and sometimes stopped my anti-depressants when I thought I could cope by myself, but I just screwed up my body even more and I think I made the depression go on longer than it might have done. From now on, I'll take the advice I'm given and stop being so bloomin' independent and proud!

'Some advice I would like to offer any new mother is to expect to feel emotional and exhausted after the birth – your hormone levels have sunk and your energy has been zapped. Don't feel guilty if you take one look at the baby and then want to nod off instead of aching to breastfeed and cuddle it. Both are normal. Do not feel that you should automatically know everything and be able to cope all of the time. When you are in hospital, the staff are there to help. Swallow your pride and ask for help! Get plenty of rest when the baby sleeps – just do the essentials and grab reinforcements when you can.

'Don't accept visitors because you feel you should. Listen to advice, but make your own decisions. Use your health visitors – they have oodles of tips. If you are feeling low and weepy after the first week – get help. Don't dwell on the fear of PND – it does happen to some of us. Don't constantly feel guilty – no parent is perfect, so don't strive too hard.'

Pippa

'I was naïve enough to think that parentcraft classes were about parenting. I was told every child is different, but there must be some common strain. Why don't they *tell* you how to cope with the more usual problems, like crying, colic, lack of sleep and extreme exhaustion? Some general advice would have really helped, but I didn't get anything. They tell you so much beforehand, and only a little bit after. After the birth it is like a wasteland – you are left alone. I feel very resentful towards the NHS for that.

'It would help if the first three months of having a baby were covered in the ante-natal classes, and then, if a further two sessions after the child is born were arranged, to prepare you for the next stages. The support I got from my health visitor has been considerable. I am much indebted to her. I didn't have much advice from anyone else.

'I do have one friend whose child is just one month older than Callum. She has helped me with emotional support, and gives me information about her child which, because of the small age gap, is often, for me, one month's advance advice. It's great, as I can use her information – forewarned, etc. It is nice to know that she is there.'

The following advice that Pippa offers really helped her through her post-natal depression. 'Speak to your doctor or health visitor – ask for help. You don't have to leave your home for help – they can visit you. Try to speak to the community psychiatric nurse, find out about and attend your local PND support group, try to get a referral to a psychiatrist. Visit friends to get away from your home environment. Join the NCT. You are already involved in this book! Talk, talk, talk – you'd be surprised just how much better you feel sharing your problems and concerns with others, and you might even get some useful advice!'

Laura

'There were no self-help groups that I was made aware of while I was ill. No doctors, surgeries or clinics with information on PND – it's like there's some taboo label on it and no one's allowed to talk about it. My local clinics are just beginning to increase awareness about PND, but not soon enough.

'I always knew that I didn't want to return to full-time work while Hannah was young because I had spent those five months in hospital and felt I had missed out on a big chunk of her early childhood. (Now, every moment spent with her is important to me.) And so I decided, instead of going back to paid work, I would set up a post-natal illness support group, run from home. The group has gone from strength to strength and is proving to be an asset to our local community.

'I now have the best of both worlds – in the mornings while Hannah is at nursery school, I get to spend time working with women who have PND (a subject very close to my heart!). I may visit them or have a meeting with other voluntary agencies, and in the afternoons, I get to spend quality time with Hannah.

'At a conference I attended some months ago, the Edinburgh Post-Natal Depression Scale (see page 127–128) was mentioned, which is a way of charting a mother's state of mental health to determine whether or not she has PND. I would also, in the future, like to campaign for more mother and baby units, implementing scales such as the EPDS, and continuing to increase awareness. I believe this illness should have the recognition it so rightly deserves and be put on the map for good.

'My group will hopefully ensure that women should not have to suffer in silence any more – and this will no longer be the "*forgotten illness*". For anyone out there suffering, I would like to offer the following advice:

COPING WITH PND: THE TEN COMMANDMENTS
Don'ts

1. If your symptoms include panic or anxiety attacks, *don't* read about ways of trying to stop these – if you can't stop them, the frustration of trying

to will intensify them. Let them come, frightening as they might seem at the time – *they will not harm you.*

2. *Don't* be the hero. If you feel uncomfortable because there are too many people coming and going, then say so. You might not be *so* tired if you hadn't had a stream of visitors all day.

3. *Don't* try and hide how you feel from your health visitor (plumping up pillows and spring-cleaning in front of her!). Remember, she is on *your* side. She will not try and take your baby away from you because you admit that you have a problem or are finding it hard to cope. Make it known how you feel.

4. *Don't* spend too much time on your own. Things always seem more severe when you're alone and have time to think. If you do spend time on your own, put the TV or radio on – a little light relief does help.

5. *Don't* read too much on medication relating to PND or other mental illnesses because there is a tendency to want to try it all. Try and let your GP or consultant guide you on these intricate matters.

Do's

1. *Do* try and find a group, or a person involved with a PND support group, or a contact number. If you haven't got the head for it, get your partner or a friend to look one up for you. If there isn't one in your locality, refer to "Useful Addresses" at the end of this book. There is always someone who can help. Remember, you are not on your own. One in ten women suffer from this illness every year.

2. *Do* try and eat or drink something. Even a nourishment drink is better than nothing. Our brains need food – don't let's deny them it.

3. *Do* try and get some rest. If someone offers to have the baby during the day, allow them to do so, and relax. I guarantee your baby will not forget you while it's out of your sight, and it most certainly won't do it any harm. It's not necessary to sleep – maybe have a coffee and read a magazine.

4 *Do* try and keep a diary on how you are feeling. When you are having a bad day, it is reassuring to read an entry for a "good day" and remember there *is* a light at the end of your tunnel.

5. *Do* try and remember that we are very impatient people – so be patient. The road to recovery is not a straight one. The good days will eventually outweigh the bad. You will most definitely get better, and will come out of it stronger than ever before.'

Gail

'I feel the way I was treated by the doctor in my pregnancy and by the hospital during and after my labour all contributed to the fact that I got PND. I felt alone and afraid. There should have been far more support and practical help available. More should have been said about PND – I hardly knew of its existence, let alone the symptoms, for weeks. I thought I was brain-damaged or going insane. People should be made more aware and professionals should not treat it so lightly. It is really important to talk when you've got this, and nobody seemed to want to listen to me.

'I found it a real help to talk to mothers who had actually suffered with it. I get very cross that it is classed as a mental illness. My doctor said it was a hormone imbalance, but still insisted on giving me those rotten anti-depressant pills. Mothers I have met who suffered from PND all seem to have brilliantly behaved babies, so it can't be the stress of them that triggered it.

'Another thing I've found is that they were all told there was something wrong – Down's, cystic fibrosis, heart trouble – only to find out afterwards that it was a mistake. I feel this may be a trigger and makes you unable to bond with a baby you feel may die.

'My husband always said that there was a reason for my suffering from PND. I thought he was bonkers and I was just damn unlucky. He has proved me wrong – he is so right. My illness has inspired me to set up my own self-help group. I am writing a poetry book about depression, I am fund-raising for the Association of Post-Natal Illness, and generally striving to make people more aware of the existence of this much suffered and much ignored illness.

'Most importantly, I strongly believe PND is due to a hormonal imbalance and should be treated as such. I am currently on a research programme via King's College Hospital, London, that will hopefully prove this theory.'

Jenny

'I was definitely depressed and I feel that it was a hormonal problem. I would like to acknowledge that I was very low during my pregnancy, and what I should have done at the time was let all that anger out about getting pregnant. I didn't because I wanted to be seen as a very caring, coping mother who managed any situation. I couldn't face the side of me that wanted to reject this baby and get on with my own life and needs. I was "one of the best mums around"! How easy it is to see things, in retrospect. A lot of my feelings were very scary at the time – feelings I had never experienced before, new to me. In a strange way, none of those feelings were wasted. The experience has made me realize that I am a much more fallible person than I thought I was, helped me to grow, to understand people better and to be more sympathetic.

'I went to relaxation classes (they were like an oasis in the desert) to help with my tenseness and inability to sleep. They were so good that I am now teaching relaxation myself, as an offshoot of this period in my life.

'Before I fell pregnant, I was considering going back to work once my second child went to full-time school. I think this potential gap was a blow to me. One male friend said to me, when he knew I was pregnant, "Well, that's another five years down the pan." This affected me very badly and I took it to heart. I did return to work when my youngest was two, which made a great deal of difference to how I was feeling. It is so nice to be "you" and not just someone's mother or wife.

'I think that the only false expectations of motherhood were my own – I had very high expectations for myself as a mother and a person, and they had to drop quite a lot. It is important not to blame your baby – it is not its fault. Quite accidentally, my eldest daughter (14 years old) saw the original draft of this and was very upset. She intuitively knew that I was not myself during this period, and I had to very carefully explain to her that in no way should one blame the baby (her younger sister) for what I went through (however tempting at the time) – it was me and my reactions that were the problem, and this only became clear as time went by.

'Finally, I feel that mothers, however bad they are feeling, should be encouraged to do as much as they can for the baby, both for the sake of bonding and for the baby's sake. Do not blame the baby, and handle it as much as possible so as to build up your relationship. Handing it over to all and sundry can set up insecurities in the baby, making it more difficult to handle in the long term for the mother. So, however tempting it is to dump the baby on someone else, I do not believe it is a good thing.

'I feel sure that some of the professionals need better training – especially midwives and health visitors.'

Sarah

'It would be wonderful if this book were to prove the catalyst for a campaign which would champion the interests of new mothers and babies, to help create a society which understood and supported without patronizing or condemning.

'What I don't understand is how little tolerance and support there is in our society for new mothers. We are expected to treat childbirth as if it were akin to buying a new washing-machine – it takes a while to find out how to work the controls and you may have to move the furniture around to fit it in, but it shouldn't have any more impact than that, and if it does then there is an assumption that the mother and father are not coping as they should. We frown at pushchairs, at messy eaters, at crying babies; they get in the way and disturb us.

'This relates very much to the macho world we live in.

'It has been recognized in Parliament and the workplace that men have created a society that requires regimentation and long hours. It is a society that, today, with our millennial lifestyle, many men find as uncomfortable as do women.

'How I long for a supportive social environment where it is expected that, for a few years at least (and without it appearing a weakness or something to be pitied), we will feel tired and vulnerable. A society where people will *smile* at our babies when they begin to get "difficult" – and then our babies will stop being "difficult" because we tolerate, even welcome, their exuberance and inquisitiveness. They will become less frustrated by worried mothers who are afraid of the social stigma of not being sufficiently controlling.

'I developed an image of myself as a new mother: suddenly I was poor, I was working-class, my clothes were cheap and stained with vomit and mucus, I was ignored and treated with disdain. This was the image which was reflected back to me as I continued my daily round: I was no longer respected or offered the same kind of service in shops and restaurants; suddenly I had no power – as a consumer of social services, of health services, of financial services. Mail order and home delivery services became my salvation.

'Finally, I always thought that anyone who moved house when pregnant or having just had a baby was mad. Having done exactly that, I now know that I was right! Pregnancy and birth are enough upheaval without adding a new environment, however desirable that environment might be, until baby is at least two years old.'

Veritee

'I feel the problem is the treatment of PND – not the fact that women get it.

'I feel that PND has always existed but that the medical people involved with PND women do not have a clue how to deal with it, and perhaps do not want to have to deal with it. I feel many have difficulties accepting that a process which society thinks should be a natural and joyful experience can make some women distressed and ill. They blame the individual woman for being somehow defective, instead of treating PND as a part of the process for an awful lot of mothers.

'I feel that some male doctors may feel subconsciously guilty for a condition that they as men are partly responsible for – pregnancy and childbirth – but experience few of the discomforts of. They therefore want it to be an easy, natural process and are blind to the difficulties.

'This will not change until these points are taken on board:

1. PND must be recognized as a specific illness with a specific cause – having a baby. My experience was that no one wanted to accept that I had PND.

2. Whatever your medical history, whether you have had mental health problems before or not, you should be regarded the same as everyone else, though perhaps professionals should be more alert to the fact that you might get PND if you are prone to depression. Nevertheless, they should be alert with every woman.

3. Any woman can get PND. It does not mean you are in any way weak or inadequate, or have somehow failed to cope with having a child. I think some professionals – doctors, health visitors, etc. – have this attitude towards depressed women.

4. However, how you cope with PND and the form your symptoms take are influenced by how you feel about being a parent, and any vulnerabilities, fears, unresolved feelings or unfinished issues from childhood, and beyond, will be exaggerated. So therapy can help, but it must be therapy based on the recognition that you have PND and it must be used to reduce the stress of a very real situation.

5. PND, I repeat, is an illness probably in part hormone-based. My PND certainly felt that way, as it has got better gradually as my body has gone back to normal. The more my cycle regulates, the better I feel, and this for me has taken seven years without treatment. I think the illness can be shortened with treatment.

6. Because of the above (point 5), PND must be regarded as different from other clinical depressions as it has a specific cause and, I believe, a *self-limiting duration* that is different for each woman. However, because it has a physical cause factor, treatment can be long and not always successful. Therefore, some emphasis must be placed on relieving the symptoms and the stress caused and helping the woman to cope.

7. Women suffering from post-natal depression often express a fear of harming their children. It does absolutely no good to them to have a system whereby if they do express this fear, then straightaway the child protection authorities and Social Services jump in, threatening to take the child away. Women are terrified of expressing any fears, in case this should happen. I believe few women do actually harm their children – it is probably more likely that they would harm themselves.

   All this could be avoided if PND was recognized enough for there to be a specialist PND team in each area consisting of health professionals, counsellors, etc. If this existed, a woman with PND would be regarded differently from other cases of potential child abuse and from other depressed people, and be more likely to get the kind of treatment that she needs. It would also be an opportunity for women to air their fears openly without the added worry of Social Services descending like a ton of bricks.

For a post-natally ill mother to feel that she is going to harm her child shows just how seriously ill she is. She should not, then, be treated as the child's enemy, thus making her feel even worse. She is the one who needs the comfort, care and support.

8. Any intervention must regard the mother and child as one unit. The woman has PND only because she has had this child. *The two are completely interlinked.* All through my experience, I was told that the Social Services, the paediatrician, the health visitor, etc. were not interested in me and my well-being, but only in the baby. This had the effect of making me feel guilty for having needs too. (Shouldn't my whole life just be about caring for this child? – that was the message.) This alienated me further from my child and also helped to further destroy my failing self-image – that is, I was no longer important now I'd had a baby.

    All this did not help the child. The best person to look after a young child is its parent. And the parent needs to be helped to do this.

9. However, none of the above is any good at all if PND is not diagnosed or recognized in the first place. Apparently, if I'd had the mental health Social Services team involved and not the child protection team, the way I was treated would have been quite different. However, no one involved with me even mentioned the term PND, let alone suggested that I had it. They did suggest that I was depressed, but this did not make any sense to me at the time as I had suffered from clinical depression prior to ever having children, and for me the symptoms were different. I now know that what I was suffering from was the illness post-natal depression.

'If you think you are suffering from PND, get in touch with the Association for Post-Natal Illness as soon as possible. Talking to a mother who has been through it and is now all right can really help. The fact that any contact is on the telephone and you never have to meet the person face to face is helpful. You can tell them all the worst things and it will go no further.

'Get other treatment which you feel will be right for you. This can be therapy, drugs, hospitalization, counselling – whatever you feel you need. And get it as soon as you realize something is wrong.

'I used to feel guilty if I felt like a sleep in the middle of the day. A counsellor told me to be kind to myself – I deserved to have treats and a rest. I now take whatever rest I can whenever I need it and can manage it. I recommend it for everyone.

'Take one day at a time. If you have a bad day do not let it spoil the next one.

'Get treatment as soon as you can, and take time off from work sick if you need to.

'Get help around the house any way you can, if you need it. I could not afford to pay very much so I offered a single mother free accommodation in return for childcare. We helped each other.

'Ask other parents to look after your children sometimes. Do not be worried to ask. Remember, if they are not ill they do not feel like you feel. When you are ill it is difficult to see that other mothers might even enjoy having another child round for the day – especially after the age of three, when they enjoy playing with each other. Do not worry about leaving your children. They enjoy the experience of being with others as long as you come back.

'Try to assert what you need. Write your needs down so as to get things clearer. Then take them to the people that can help – spouse, friends, relatives, doctor, health visitor, counsellor, and so on.

'P.S. I always wanted to write this book myself, but somehow never felt well enough or had the time. That is why I am so pleased to be able to contribute my story, and I hope it will be used. I think that to publish stories of many women's PND is one way to get recognition of the problem and to publicize possible ways to help. It will also reassure a lot of women that they are not alone, that their symptoms are common to sufferers, and that it will get better.'

15

The Myth of Perfect Mothering

Having worked on this book for the past three years, I almost feel as though I have spent a lifetime researching the subject of post-natal depression. I have interviewed and spoken to hundreds of women who have suffered from this terrible and neglected illness. I am no longer shocked by anyone's story, but truly and deeply saddened each time I hear, in every single case, of the all too common feeling of total isolation.

I have been able to link many common symptoms with PND, but the one which stands out in every story is that each and every woman felt convinced at the time that she was the only one in the world experiencing her awful thoughts and feelings.

I have read book upon book of theories on why we suffer from PND. Many say that it is totally hormone-related. Others insist that it is because the mother has a previous history of mental illness. And then, it is said that PND is a 'circumstantial illness'. I presume that my theory fits into that category, because the word 'circumstantial' leaves the mind wide open to a million different 'circumstances' which could be the cause.

My personal opinion is that post-natal depression is due to the *myth of perfect mothering*, which I have broken down into various components. I have also stated my opinion on how this could all change for the future generation of mums.

As mothers, we all seem to have the same high self-expectations when it comes to motherhood. I have time and again asked myself why, and have concluded that these are the four contributing factors:

1. the media image of motherhood
2. society's attitude
3. our own parents' influence
4. effects from our own childhood.

1. The media image of motherhood

The media paint a very pretty picture of motherhood – always a smiling mother and a squeaky-clean baby. This is not usually the case, but we inevitably prepare ourselves for this image and try to live up to it.

2. Society's attitude

At the mother and toddler groups I attended, the conversations were filled with comparisons about whose baby was doing what, whose was sleeping through the night, which babies were taking solids, drinking 7 oz bottles, whose was saying this, whose was crawling, walking, etc. The mothers would all say (whether true or not) that they were totally fulfilled by their role. It seemed as though every mother there had an image to project: that they were coping well and enjoying every minute of motherhood. Following the joyful account of woman number one, woman number two would say that she was coping well, woman number three would go one step further and say she was ecstatic, and woman number four would chant on about having another six babies.

I wondered what would happen if I had piped up, 'I hate this job, my baby screams, doesn't sleep, I cannot cope, I'm bored and feeling depressed.' Would everyone have turned their back on me or would the next woman have said, 'Actually, I feel a bit like that too?' Instead, we all continued to pretend that we were happy and well.

Perhaps a mother and baby group which specifically advertised for the mother who is not enjoying her role or finding it difficult would be a good idea. Or perhaps a group should exist for the ex-career women who now find themselves at home all day with their babies but still need stimulating company.

3. Our own parents' influence

Our parents seem to have very short memories. Although in some cases they can be sympathetic, they too project an image of 'perfect parenting'.

When we scream or cry and seem unable to cope, they are always ready to tell us to be just that bit more patient, that the children grow up all too quickly, that these are the best years of our lives. They never screamed, they coped well.

This doesn't help. I often wish that I could turn the clocks back and observe members of my family after they had had a sleepless night coupled with a constantly whingeing child, a sick baby, not to mention the other constant demands on their time. Perhaps this would enlighten us to the fact that we are really quite normal in the way we react.

I promise my children that when I am a grandparent, I will admit to my screaming, tantrums and tears if they ever need that bit of moral support. It may not help their situation, but it certainly will show them that their mum was not perfect.

4.Effects from our own childhood

There is usually something set deep within us that we strive hard to match up to, or something that we try even harder not to do.

Some of us had a 'perfect childhood' with 'perfect parents', and our aim is to give our children that same upbringing. Some of us, though, have childhood memories that don't please us. Therefore we fight against the natural similarities we have to our parents, in order to avoid inflicting the same sort of childhood memories on our own children.

These are both natural reactions once we become parents ourselves, but yet another inevitable pressure we live with.

During my research, I discovered that a very common phenomenon in women who had post-natal depression was a problematic relationship with their own parents or problems during their own childhood. During my counselling session following my episodes of PND, it transpired that many of my personal fears, insecurities, sadness and feelings of inability to cope as a mother were due to problems within my own childhood. We are the result of our upbringing, and the deepest of memories tend to unearth any problems when we become mothers ourselves. An account of my childhood experiences follows, together with the writings of other contributors who felt able to write about their own childhood.

Cara

I enjoyed my childhood but as an adult, with children of my own, memories came flooding back which definitely didn't help me when I was feeling depressed. My parents divorced when I was eleven. I have clear and sad memories of them arguing late into the night, and of how I used to will the phone to ring to break up the fight. I remember with dread the fear of my parents divorcing – it was inevitable, but the anticipation was much worse than the actuality.

Life was happier when Dad left home; the atmosphere was much better. Mum always encouraged us to see my dad frequently and welcomed him into our home – the divorce (in a child's eye) was amicable. My mum had to work extremely hard in order to pay her mortgage on our new home and meet the bills, but we had everything any child could ever wish for. My older brother and I had to become a bit more independent: Mark was now the 'man of the house', and I helped with the cooking and cleaning, etc. We all mucked in together, and life was never dull.

Since having my own children, I always try to make sure that Roo and I *never* argue when they are in earshot. That can be tough at times, especially when I have

PMT! From experience, though, I feel it would be a lot tougher on the children if they heard us fight.

My mother went through a very bad patch in her life when I was twelve. She had very recently lost her father (her first bereavement), who meant everything in the world to her. He was her 'sun, moon and stars'. He was the closest person to her in life and his sudden and unexpected death left her utterly devastated. She was given sleeping pills and tranquillizers by the doctor, to help her through this period.

Soon after, my mother was raped in her own home while I and my brother and sister were asleep. She was threatened – he would harm her children, he said – but as always, she protected us. She could not go to the police – that was made perfectly clear. The doctor gave her stronger sleeping pills and stronger tranquillizers to help her cope with her life. She was still working, struggling to make ends meet and fighting desperately to put on a brave face when she was with us.

My mother was involved with a man she deeply loved during this time. The relationship was faltering – a further devastation, and very probably the straw that broke the camel's back. Unable to cope any longer, and by now drugged up with medication, she took an overdose of pills. The memory of that night still haunts me today. It was not a selfish move on her part, it was desperation – something I have felt time and again since having depression.

Although I understand that her actions were totally beyond her control, this incident has still left me with a terrible fear of the death of the people I love. It is a subconscious fear that lurks deep in the back of my mind. When I am feeling emotionally vulnerable, I can just about cope with Roo driving to work, but I fear for my children's safety and frequently wake at night in cold sweats panicking about them – I even feel my dog's belly sometimes to make sure that she is still breathing. This is the sad repercussion of a traumatic childhood memory.

In my moments of deepest depression and desperation, I have held a bottle of pills and been so very tempted to end my life. I've planned to jump under a train or smash my car into a brick wall. I have then screamed and cried, thinking, 'I don't want history to repeat itself, my children must not suffer.'

In many ways I bear a very strong likeness to my mum, which includes a lack of patience, a need for time to 'be me', a dislike of getting down and playing with the children, and only half-listening when I am (frequently) preoccupied. All these things about my mother annoy me terribly and often make me feel as though I and the children are insignificant when we are in her company. Because of this, I am struggling very hard not to be like her – I want my children to feel needed, wanted and very significant. It is a constant and hard fight with myself – I do not always win.

I must add here that if ever I have seriously needed the best advice available, my mum has been the person to offer it. I do not want to paint a bad picture of her

– she is my very best friend. She is great fun, loves me to madness, and I can talk to her openly about anything in the world. She encourages me to have my independence and to work. She will come with me to a fairground and go on the scary rides. She will take me to nightclubs and show me that life exists after 10 p.m. – something I forgot for a short while.

But sometimes, just sometimes, I do want a 'mummy'. I begin to feel the child in me crying out for her love and affection but she, like me, is a total lunatic, tackles everything she can at once and has little time for any one person individually. It is hard for me to understand it but, as time goes by, I realize I am doing exactly the same. I then have to give myself a strong talking-to and 'put on my maternal head'!

I will always try very hard to give my girls 'mummy love' as well as friendship. When they grow up I will always remember that they are my babies, even when they have their own.

Rosemary

'Unfortunately, I could not turn to my mother for comfort during this difficult period, as our relationship has never been an easy one and I felt that she was at least partly to blame for the situation I was in. Before I begin describing why I felt and continue to feel deeply resentful towards her, I should say, in order to be fair, that she always meant well and has a number of very positive qualities. However, as a mother she was oppressively domineering to the degree that even as teenagers we were not entitled to an opinion truly our own and were expected to conform to her wishes, even including what we were to wear at any given moment.

'Actually, she has never tried to really get to know who myself or my sister really are, but sees life in accordance with how people are supposed to behave.

'She has always firmly believed, and still does, that the only source of happiness and meaning in a woman's life is to be married and have children and to continue to see her own mother as the endless source of genuine wisdom. However, she was deeply unhappy in her own marriage and constantly complained to us about our father and how all other men, apart from him, were wonderful. She would even compare all the other men of our acquaintance, whether they were neighbours or relatives, claiming they were wonderful husbands, and moan about how other wives did not suffer what she suffered. Actually, my father was no different from any other; he was a perfectly normal man in most ways with a number of good qualities, but had the usual male failings, including lack of affection. Their marriage was a disaster simply because they were totally unsuited.

'However, despite my mother's own experiences, she constantly drummed into us the absolute necessity of getting married, which in practice made me feel worthless in myself. When I reached 22 years old she metaphorically hit the panic button and pointed at any male as being perhaps a suitable husband. All my successes academically seemed to be of no great importance to her. This was in the early seventies, when women were supposed to be at last liberated from the nonsense of finding Prince Charming as the ultimate goal of their lives. However, despite the fact that I had an excellent career, I obviously could not shake myself free of her influence and the need to do as she said. I married, I know, to a great degree to please her and to stop her nagging me.

'Having the baby was the same thing all over again. No sooner were we a few months married than she started pressuring me to have babies, and even took my husband aside and told him to get on with it as her great ambition was to be a grandmother!

'So I had the babies, the process hastened by the fact that for physical reasons I was advised to do so early. Throughout my pregnancy and the difficulties with my daughter, I was aware that my most important source of anxiety was that if anything went wrong my mother would blame me. And so I found myself, with babies, miserable and in a foreign country without my career, which until then was the most important thing to give myself a feeling of worth. And I realized that I had done exactly the same thing as my mother: married too young, lived abroad and felt like a fish out of water. I vaguely remembered her as a young mother – all her life ironing, or so it seemed to me. For that, and her being strict and unhappy, are the most enduring memories of my childhood. It seems so stupid after all these years and at my age to still feel the resentment.

'However, even if I did not, there would still be difficulties as my mother lives mentally in another world – that of Victorian England – and we simply cannot have a genuine conversation. I tried a few times to speak as myself, but she either did not understand at all or got offended. We are just too different and cannot, unfortunately, have a real conversation. That creates tension, and being with her is just a major strain for me – a pity, as I know she would like a close relationship with me, but she is totally incapable of it.'

Julie

Julie was born in Australia and had an older brother. When she was three, she and her mother moved back to England, leaving behind her brother and father. Her mother later explained to Julie that her brother had died of leukaemia.

When Julie was six, her mother remarried and Julie was legally adopted by her stepfather. A year later she had a new baby sister. From this point on, Julie was given a lot of unfair 'parental' responsibility, which included having to take the baby out for long walks and settle her at night with a story. 'I have a vague memory of being in her bedroom one night and she was crying and crying. My head hurt so much, and in frustration I hit the side of the cot. I was only eight myself.'

When she was nine her mother and adoptive father split up, which meant moving home with her mother and her new boyfriend. Julie was then allowed to play out at night with friends while the couple went drinking.

Her mother and her boyfriend began to argue all the time, and Julie and her sister sat up in bed at night listening to the rows and feeling very upset and frightened. Her adoptive father, who she visited weekly, had now met another woman who was nice to Julie but who she didn't like at all. She had just changed schools and her school work was suffering badly. Eventually, her mother left her new man and went back to her second husband. Julie moved schools again.

When Julie was eleven, her mother admitted to her that her brother hadn't really died but was living in Australia with her biological father, who was a schizophrenic.

As Julie grew older she was the apple of her adoptive father's eye, and her mother became increasingly jealous and spent as much time as possible putting Julie down and knocking her confidence. When she became a teenager, her mother and adoptive father restrained her beyond reason. She began to clash more with her mother, and when Julie had a boyfriend her mother would try to join in. If she changed her hairstyle, her mother changed hers. Her mother had a few minor health problems and began to play on her illnesses. Julie often had to take time out from school to help her mother at home, and took on most of the household responsibilities including all the ironing, all of the time.

Her mother ran up huge bills which they couldn't afford to pay. The debt collectors often called round, and following their visit she would take an overdose. This happened frequently.

When Julie was fifteen, she met Michael, her present husband. He got on very well with her family and even looked after her younger sister when Julie went on a school trip. Even though Julie and Michael had very strong feelings for each other, Michael respected Julie's age and never made sexual advances towards her. One night, things got pretty steamy between them but they controlled the situation. Michael explained what had happened to Julie's mother, who was delighted at his honesty and just told him to be careful in future. She called him 'son', and appeared to be very understanding.

Soon after this, Julie was told that she couldn't, under any circumstances, see Michael any more and was even threatened with a court order by her parents. She later discovered that her mother had purposely led her adoptive father to believe that Julie and Michael were sexually involved.

Julie left school and found a job. She paid half of her wages to her mother but still took on the majority of the household chores even though her mother was at home all day playing her CB radio. She dated a couple of times, but still loved and missed Michael. When she was seventeen, she started seeing him secretly. This was discovered and her adoptive father, after giving her a terrible telling-off, one mealtime pushed her plate in her face and broke her nose.

Her mother seemed to be enjoying all this, which didn't help matters. Julie's life became full of humiliation and mental torture, her front-door key was taken away and the restrictions began all over again. She began to feel so depressed about her life and at one time even considered taking an overdose. At this stage, she decided to move away from home and became totally rejected by her parents. She contacted Michael and they later got engaged. They married just after Julie's nineteenth birthday. None of her family attended the wedding.

Over the years Julie always sent her younger sister birthday cards and gifts, but they were ripped up and returned. Her sister was too young to know what had truly been going on over the years, and had been told a lot of lies and believed them. Julie was not there to defend herself.

A few years later, Julie's mother arrived on her doorstep with the news that her biological father had been in touch from Australia and wanted to meet Julie. She met him, listened to his unhappy life story and heard that her older brother was a drug dealer who had left his wife and children. Julie found her father to be unstable and strange and chose not to see him again. Her brother later arrived very briefly on the scene, telling Julie that he had been sexually abused by their father but didn't think that Julie had been.

Julie later fell pregnant and had her daughter Sarah. Her mother then wanted to make up. But Julie knew that her mother would never really change and that each time, over the years, that she had opened herself up to her mother, she became even more hurt. Her mother threatened with legal action to see the baby and make Julie's life hell.

From this point on, Julie wished her mother dead. She had completely ruined her life so far.

Julie's family is now her husband, daughter and in-laws.

'I'm not a trained psychologist, but I'm intelligent enough to analyse things up to a point – some things are logical. No one really seems to know what causes post-natal depression, but hormonal changes, brain chemistry problems, stress and loss of a mother or problems with a mother–daughter relationship have been mentioned. I'm sure that the problems I had must have affected me. I did miss having a mum of my own when I was pregnant (although I must stress that Michael's mum was brilliant). I tried so hard not to be like my own mother, but obviously genetically there are some likenesses that I can't change. She caused me emotional stress after the birth, when I could have done without extra pressure. Each time I do something like her or sound like her, I cringe. Maybe I didn't take to motherhood so well because of the kind of mother I'd had. The responsibilities she placed on me at a young age wouldn't have helped. I resented looking after a baby then, which may make me do so now sometimes.

'The one good thing to come out of all this, though, is that I will make sure that I don't push my daughter away, ever. This will of course cause me stress, though. I know I will still try too hard to be the perfect mum, or what I think a perfect mum should be.'

Laura

'Any relationship is difficult to have – those between parents and children, husband and wife and even friends.

'While I was going through this illness, it came to light that my own mother had also suffered from a form of post-natal illness. Unfortunately, 30 years ago it was not recognized as PND, but as a mother being neurotic. She was prescribed Valium and told to go home and get on with it. It must have been a nightmare. Even midwives were not clued up, so there was no available support.

'I think, with hindsight, I would have preferred to know about my own mother's illness, then, just maybe, I might have been able to have some sort of preventive treatment or therapy. It is very difficult for either of my parents to deal with my illness. As with all parents nationwide, there is an enormous feeling of failure and guilt on their part, as if it were something they had done. I would not pin the blame on any one particular person, as I am an adult in my own right and have also failed myself at one point or another.

'I am now trying to build the sort of relationship with my daughter that doesn't put me on a pedestal – that basically shows I am not a superwoman and have fears and worries, and that I, too, do get upset. I think many parents make the mistake of hiding these negative emotions away when, in fact, it is these very emotions that help your child to deal with the real world.

'My daughter has seen me cry on occasions, and when she has asked me what the matter is I have told her simply that I am not happy *all* the time, and that sometimes mummies and daddies get upset. When she is old enough, I will discuss my experience with her to enable her to understand what I had to deal with. Eventually, she may herself want a family and I will do everything in my power to prevent her from having to endure all the pain and suffering I went through.'

Veritee

'I would like to say something about one particular factor to do with why I think I got PND – my relationship with my own parents. I do not believe this is the major reason I was depressed, but although without the other factors I might have got through, my relationship with my parents predisposed me to depression when I had my own child.

'My mother is a lovely woman who has always had sight problems and is now blind. But without going into details, my father was an eccentric and very strong man much liked by friends and colleagues, but an emotional tyrant at home. He used his children to try to satisfy his own emotional needs, which in fact no one could satisfy because of his own upbringing. He made me feel unsafe, and because my mother was also emotionally scared of him she was unable to make me feel safe either, as she could not protect me from him.

'I believe that when I had my own child, the child in me became scared again. How could I protect and care for my own child properly when I felt so unprotected and scared myself?

'When things started to go wrong, this scared child surfaced again and led to doubts about my own ability as a parent. It also caused me to react like a child and not like an adult mother of a new baby. When people started to intervene in my life, I was unable to assert what was right for myself and my child. But I don't think this caused my depression. The usual factors, especially the change in hormones, are enough to tip a new mother over the edge. However, when your whole life is founded on such a shaky base it is impossible to keep your balance when your life is rocked.'

The reality of motherhood

These are the factors that strike me most forcibly as characterizing motherhood:

1. total lack of experience of it
2. ignorance of it
3. absence of preparation or lessons in motherhood
4. loss of youth and freedom (inner change)
5. shedding of your past identity
6. abrupt end to your own childhood
7. need to adapt to the responsibility of motherhood
8. having to learn to share all over again.
9. a major shock and transition
10. change of routine
11. lack of sleep
12. loss of energy.

Having a baby equals a sudden and dramatic change to your life. Despite all the preparation during the ante-natal period, giving birth itself is a traumatic and exhausting experience. Being presented with a new-born child can be a great shock. Once it is born, you have a twenty-four-hour responsibility for life.

Without a doubt, we are all, to a certain extent, self-centred. A new-born baby zaps your energy, demands constant attention and takes away your identity as an individual.

I believe that post-natal depression can be brought on by this total shock to your life. I think that the adaptation to motherhood is totally underestimated – we were never made aware of how hard it would be and we were *never* warned about post-natal illness.

All this could be prevented if we were given a comprehensive lesson in motherhood, which would consist of the following pointers:

1. Learn to share.

2. Learn to give without return.

3. Be prepared to lose something of yourself.

4. Be prepared to be totally responsible for another human being's life.

5. Accept that you will be in constant demand.

6. Be prepared to take second, third or fourth place.

7. Be prepared to lose a lot of sleep – to live with exhaustion.

8. Be prepared to live in a 'stiff upper lip' environment.

9. Watch out for the signs of PND.

10. If you think you are depressed contact your GP immediately.

If such a lesson could be taught, perhaps in the form of a list of inevitabilities and warnings, we as women would truly be prepared for the worst scenario of motherhood. This simple list could be available via ante-natal clinics or midwives, or even distributed in the last year of school. It might even prompt teenagers to use reliable contraception and would definitely highlight the realities of motherhood in contrast to the existing myth. Literature which tells the truth about becoming a parent and the responsibilities entailed should be made easily accessible.

While I was post-natally ill, a major symptom of my depression was feeling frequently and generally unwell. I visited my GP at least twice a week with minor ailments. The health visitors are based at the doctor's surgery and hold all the baby clinics there. Perhaps if post-natal illness had been publicized in the form of a large poster in the surgery I might have recognized, or admitted, that I was not just generally unwell but suffering from PND. Such a poster might say:

FOR 9 OUT OF 10 MOTHERS, HAVING A BABY = BLISS

FOR 1 OUT OF 10 MOTHERS, HAVING A BABY = HELL

If you are feeling tearful, emotional, unable to cope, unable to sleep, etc., etc., speak to your doctor. You may be suffering from post-natal depression. Help is available.

Another very important issue that needs to be dealt with concerns society at large. Motherhood *minus* post-natal depression is hard enough, without society condemning the actions, the behaviour, of parents and children in the way that it does. The pressure exerted on parents to turn out a 'well-behaved' child when going on an outing, for instance, puts an immense strain on the whole family before they have even left home.

Children are energy. Children are many other things, too, including noise and mess. They are also our future. The fact is that if children in this country were able to express themselves freely, there would be a more peaceful, relaxed atmosphere all round. A more supportive and accepting society, in addition to the help that doctors can give in the form of pills and hormones, would go a long way towards reducing the incidence of, and speeding up the recovery from, post-natal depression.

Finally, as every one of the contributors to this book has pointed out, awareness about PND and its implications urgently needs to be raised. It should no longer be a taboo subject – it is a severe illness which needs sympathy and the correct treatment.

If you are reading this book and you know that you are ill, do not suffer in silence. It is up to you, and only you, to speak up for yourself. When you close your door on the world tonight, just remember that at home, no one hears you scream.

16

Light at the End of the Tunnel

For the women out there who are suffering today, I feel that this is the most important chapter for you to read: you *will* recover, you *will* find yourself again – that I promise you. Just hold on tight: you will find more happiness at the end of the tunnel than you ever knew possible.

In every other chapter I have written first, but I feel that this poem written by Lynn Leahy for her own son and daughter (and first published in issue 3 of *Radical Motherhood*, is the perfect way to highlight the rewards of having children.

On Learning

I love to learn.
The desire to do so begins at my core
And seeps through my being.
I face old age – content
For I know I will still be learning,
Thus passion can never leave me.

I have had many teachers, each bringing a different lesson.
Few did I thank, I often failed to realize what they were offering
– Yet I took it still.

Of all my teachers two must be named,
For they have taught me with such good humour.
My children, you have taught me so much.

Robert, when you were born, my son,
I was daunted by the prospect of being your protector and guide through
    life.
I looked down at your squashed, bruised head and felt only panic.
How pompous I feel now to have assumed that,
For you have guided me with ease and grace.

You did not laugh at my fear of insects,
Just showed me their charms through your eyes.

'Feel, mum, how its legs tickle,' you said and I stood rigid
While the woodlouse was plonked on my hand and trooped across.
I faced the fact later, that nothing terrible had happened when you took it
back!

With you and for you, I have chased escaped rabbits across gardens and
fields (and learnt to catch them, however quick they are).
I have learnt to love even 'those gerbilly things', that hold such a place in
your heart.
I must have, I can laugh instead of rant when we cut open the sofa to
extract them
And they later escape again and eat my bedding.
We have learnt together to be midwives to guinea-pigs and been able to
marvel at the cycle of life, at such close hand.

You have helped me remember how to play.
You may not have realized, but when you were born I was forgetting how
to.
I used to swim up and down, up and down, keeping fit (for this is what
you do when you are grown up).
You helped me to believe I was a dolphin and even a seal,
And to mind less when people cast us strange looks.

Chrissy, my daughter, you have helped me to feel my delight
With you, with the world and with the girl still in me.
You demand that I show my energy and so with you I can dance with
abandon (And later justify how important it was, to keep you
company).

You are at ease being feminine and you insist now and then that I take the
trouble to be so too.
'Wear a skirt, Mummy,' you say, 'I think you look pretty like that.'
And so from you I learn to take compliments, for I could never doubt
your sincerity.
No longer am I at ease with the 'what are you after?' comments that I
brought from my youth.
Through you I have learnt to listen better, simply because you deserve me
to do so.
When I begin my 'Just a minute', 'I won't be long now' routine,
If I ever catch your eye, I see that look which says,
'Why don't you stop, mum, have you forgotten how important I am?'
And slowly I learn that things can wait.
This is such a hard lesson for me – please be patient with me.

My fear about helping you both to find a way safely through life
prompted me even to join karate with you.
ME – who up until then, could hide behind a belief I was too busy or
getting too old for 'something really physical'.
And now I 'KIE' with the rest and have been surprised
How much I enjoy showing I have strength and control.

You have both helped me to see the good and bad in myself.
'You're being unfair, Mum,' one of you tells me at times, and you say it
without rancour or put-down and so you manage to face me with the
fact that I am.

When I accuse one of you of doing something that is 'really not very
helpful' the other one helps me see that invariably they learnt it from
me.

My children, you are my favourite teachers,
I have no doubts that you understand just how much I love you,
But had you realized why I will forever be in your debt?

Cara

'GOD NEVER SENDS THE WINTER WITHOUT THE JOY OF SPRING.'

Have I found the light at the end of the tunnel, or simply a beautiful rainbow? How I would regret not having my two beautiful girls, who have filled my life with sunshine. Of course they fill my days with plenty of aggravation too, but I do love waking up each morning to see their smiling faces and big blue eyes, and inviting them into my bed for a great big cuddle. There is no better way to start my day...except on a Sunday, when I just wish they wouldn't wake me up – how I miss those lazy mornings! I look forward to their incessant chatter (unless I have a hangover or am suffering from severe PMT) and the chaos in the kitchen with conversation (and food) flying in all directions. But I appreciate even more the time when peace and quiet return, when Georgina has left for school and Tasha is busy, involved in her play world.

My light didn't truly appear until Tasha turned two. Life was hard. I had to sacrifice my true self in order to survive the earlier years. I could only keep on praying that I would emerge again, one day, in one piece. That did happen.

But, if I am totally honest with myself and you, that light still dims on a bad day when the children are nagging and I am feeling fraught. Life is never quite the same again. Once a mother...you will always worry about your child and somehow, totally unexpectedly, they take priority over every action you take. I thank my children for making me who I am today (others may not!).

Without them, I would have grown old and selfish. They have taught me to love more than I ever thought possible.

I have learnt to listen harder (and longer, at times), to appreciate a rainbow, to count the spots on a ladybird, to wrap up warm on the coldest winter's day and run in the fields (and enjoy it), to laugh, for their sakes, even if I need to cry; but most of all, to look forward to each new day.

It has most certainly been a long, hard struggle, fighting for my life at times. Now I will spend the rest of my life fighting for my children. Georgina and Tasha – you are my life and I love you both more than words could ever say.

Never, ever give up. The best is yet to come.

Rosemary

'I actually began to really enjoy my children when they were about seven years old, and the older they grew the better things got. This was because the degree of mess, noise and sheer hard work began to decrease and because the children were now people with whom I could sensibly converse. I would not have any more children – the first years are just too dreadful – but I do not regret having had them because they are such good company now.'

Jane

Jane feels that she has now reached the light at the end of the tunnel. 'We still have problems, money is always short, but in general, things are looking up. I am able to enjoy being with the children and plan and look forward to the future. Both Daisy and Jacob are happy, outgoing children. My life and interests are very different from the way they were before the children were born, but I am content in my role as a mother. I never regret having my children – my only regret is that I haven't been able to enjoy them when they were babies. It's only been from when they were about one year old that I could start to relax and get pleasure out of being with them. Also, I would love to have more children, but at the moment I feel that the risk of becoming ill again is not worth taking. I feel that it would be unfair to subject Paul and the children to the possibility of a further episode of PND.

'I really would love to have a baby and actually enjoy it. Perhaps I will foster or adopt when Daisy and Jacob are older.

'I now try to help people I come into contact with to realize that, although PND can be devastating, with time, support and (sometimes) medication it is possible to enjoy life again.'

Julie

'Yes, there *is* light at the end of the tunnel. It may seem to fade at times, but its bright beam keeps you going. Of course there is still frustration at times, but I couldn't live without Sarah. I feel that as she is growing older, we can communicate better, and in turn, I feel like I'm being a better mum. I couldn't even imagine hurting myself or ending my life now as I did when I was ill.

'I couldn't bear to miss Sarah growing up.

'No one could have prepared me for the strength of feeling there is between a child and its mother. Practically, you do get into better routines, and with each new developmental stage come new hurdles to jump but with more fulfilment and enjoyment. I still yell like a madwoman when I'm tired and Sarah is naughty – I still wish I could be supermum and do still feel guilty sometimes.

'Watching Sarah grow and learn is amazing – even after a hard day at work when I'm totally stressed out, when she gives me a squeeze, wants me to play, or lets slip a "naughty word", it makes me feel that it has all been worth it as it brings a smile to my face and a flutter to my heart.

'Sarah is a little shining angel, with stardusted eyes and a cheeky smile to light up the darkest night.'

Pippa

'I keep getting glimpses of light now, but the path twists and turns and from time to time I lose sight of it. I know I will get there, but when? Not knowing how long the PND was going to last was a big problem – I really needed to know when the hell it was going to end. I got quite hung up on it.

'Now Callum is almost 18 months old and quite a little personality. He's a warm, sensitive and loving child who loves to play and laugh. I allow myself, every now and then, that luxurious thought that maybe I didn't and/or haven't made such a bad job of this parenting lark – so far, anyway.

'I have continued to have help from the CPN and the psychiatrist and am still on the anti-depressants, but have just started to reduce the dosage. Thanks to my health visitor, I have sessions at the Family Centre and am going to do a Veritas parenting programme [this teaches positive parenting skills] soon – I have the book and have seen the video, but want to do it again in a group situation so that I can hear others' views and advice. I feel that this will bring it to life. My confidence is slowly coming back and I feel that the tunnel exit is close by. The light comes from Callum's smile, his kisses and his hugs. His laugh is a breath of fresh air and something I can't get enough of. He goes to a private nursery school two half-days a week – it's our breathing space. Face it, we all need it.

'Don't get me wrong, there are still times when I can hardly wait until he goes to sleep at night! There are times when John's words about "accepting you don't know what you're doing and getting used to that idea" still ring in my ears. Now, though, I can hear the birdsong over those words and notice the flowers bloom. But that's what happens when you're head and shoulders out of the mire.'

Laura

'I was very concerned at the time that my relationship with Hannah would be affected, but on the contrary. Our relationship is so strong, even though we may have "bonded" at a very late stage. We now have an incredible bond. We are all very close and my time with Hannah is very precious indeed. When we go out shopping, it is like having a little friend with me.

'This experience has had its long-term effects on the way I feel about myself. I would have preferred it without the pain and depression, but it happened, and something most definitely positive has come out of it.

'Although this experience will stay with me for the rest of my life, I now know there was a reason for my irrational feelings and utter despair – feelings of inadequacy as a mother – and odd behaviour. It was because I was very ill and not because I was a bad wife and mother. Through my experience I would like to help others and ensure that my daughter will never go through all the pain and suffering I endured. She and my husband are very special to me and I will always love them.'

Gail

'I love motherhood now. It is the best thing that has ever happened to me. There aren't enough hours in the day to do all that I want to do. I'm finally back to the weight I was when I got pregnant, with slightly saggy boobies and a small, neat scar to show for what has happened. My husband has been a complete rock all through these bad times and I now love him even more, if that is at all possible. I've learnt through this illness and feel I'm a better person because of it.

'I'm much closer to my mother as she was such a help when I was low. I love life. I love my children. I love my husband.

'I'm going to have another baby sometime in the future. And I'm ready to take you on, PND, should you descend again, and once again I know I'll win!'

Jenny

'The baby is the best thing that ever happened to me – that is, as well as my other two children. The baby is one of the delights of our life and maybe, just maybe, I appreciate her and have such fun with her because we got through those difficult times together. Other mothers need to know that the bad things *will* fade and life will get better.'

Sarah

Matthew was three in December and he is now attending nursery school on a full-time basis. He is extremely happy there and Michael shares the responsibility of Matthew when he is at home. Sarah has been able to resume her interests, but still feels that this is 'survival time' right now.

She has become much tougher on her husband and, whereas she used to look after him constantly in order for him to be able to look after her in return, she now realizes that she must find the time and space for herself. 'This is a left-over from my childhood and the relationship I had with my mother. I now realize that I can no longer physically and emotionally carry the whole burden myself. I will not be having any more children now, but mainly because of Michael's wishes.'

Sarah insists that she is still not the person she used to be, but she is trying to 'get on with it' and find herself again. She feels like she has become a new person, has severed all links with her past life and is trying to discover who she is and what she wants.

'I love Matthew very much and can now honestly say that I actually miss him during the day. He is the bee's knees!'

Veritee

'I really do feel fine most of the time now. I counsel for the Association for Post-Natal Illness and I hope I help others. I have a lifestyle many would envy. I live in a big house in a beautiful part of the country with ponies to ride, a lovely view and enough friends. Caja (which means "daisy" in Cornwall) is such a wonderful child and so independent. She is now seven and appears to be happy, secure and undamaged by my depression.

'When Caja was four and a half years old, it was discovered by the school doctor that she had a heart murmur. It had never been noted in the paediatrician's records that this was the case. I do not know if they knew about it, but it would most certainly explain her frailty and failure to thrive. I more recently went to see a heart specialist who explained that, more than likely, Caja has always had it. At first it was thought to be a hole in her heart but now it is known to be a valve defect. She is currently undergoing further investigations and may have to have repair surgery in the future. I, as Caja's mother, always knew something was wrong, but no one listened to me. Her condition can only be detected by listening to her neck, and in Caja's notes, when she was seeing the doctors regularly for her failure to thrive, it stated normal heart sounds. This now explains why she never thrived as a baby. Everyone just blamed me – they were blinded by the conviction that I was a neglectful mother, although they could never pinpoint it.

'I would love to have another child. If I was younger, I would have waited and had another baby once Caja reached this age. I resent the fact that by not having treatment for PND at the right time it took a lot longer to recover, and now a baby seems out of the question. I have not got time, I feel too old, and I am also too scared in case this all happened again. I realize only too well that it would be hard with two children and I would have to give up work.

'My other motivation for having another child would be to put right what went wrong. I would love to give birth the natural way. I have always wanted to give birth like this, but have never been able to find out what it is like. It would not be fair on a child to have one for those reasons, though.'

Useful Addresses

Association of Breastfeeding Mothers
PO Box 441, St Albans
Herts AL4 0AS
Tel: 020 8778 4769

The Association for Post-Natal Illness
25 Jerdan Place
London SW6 1BE
Tel: 020 7386 0868

Cry-sis (for parents suffering from a crying baby)
BM Cry-sis
London WC1N 3XX
Tel: 020 7404 5011

Gingerbread Association (for one-parent families)
35 Wellington Street
London WC2E 7BN
Tel: 020 7240 0953

Home-Start UK (voluntary domestic support)
2 Salisbury Road
Leicester LE1 7QR
Tel: 0116 233 9955

MAMA (Meet a Mum Association)
Waterside centre
26 Avenue Road
South Norwood
London SE25 4DX
Tel: 020 8771 5595
Helpline: 020 8768 0123 (Monday to Friday 7pm to 10pm)

Marce Society
c/o Dr Trevor Friedmann
Department of Psychiatry, Leicester General Hospital
Leicester LE5 4PN
Tel: 0116 249 0440

MIND (The National Association for Mental Health)
22 Harley Street
London W1N 2ED
Tel: 020 7637 0741

The Miscarriage Association
18 Stoneybrook Close, West Bretton
Wakefield WF4 4TP
Tel: 01924 200 799
PO Box 24, Ossett,
West Yorkshire WF5 9XG
Tel: 01924 830515

NCT (National Childbirth Trust)
Alexandra House, Oldham Terrace
London W3 6NH
Tel: 020 8992 8637

PMS Help
PO Box 160, St Albans
Herts AL1 4UQ

PMT Advisory Service
PO Box 268, Hove
East Sussex BN3 1RW
Tel: 01273 771366

The Samaritans
17 Uxbridge Road, Slough
Berks SL1 1SN
Tel: 01753 32713
A 24-hour service for those who feel desperate or suicidal (see also local telephone book)

SANDS (Stillbirth and Neonatal Death Society)
Argyle House, 29–31 Euston Road
London NW1 2SD
Tel: 020 7833 2851

Support Group for Carers of PND
Mrs C. McKenna
8 Broomfield, East Goscote
Leicestershire LE7 3XY

Useful websites
Offering information about PND and contact with other sufferers on-line.
http://www.pni.org.uk
http://www.jkp.com

References

Ballad, C.G., Stanley, A.K. and Brockington, I.F. (1995) 'Post traumatic stress disorder following childbirth.' *British Journal of Psychiatry 166*, 525–528.

Boileau de Costelnau, P. (1861) 'Misopedie ou Lesion de l'amour de la progeniture.' *Annales Medico-psychologiques 7*, 553–568.

Emerson, S. (1987) *A Celebration of Babies.* New York: Dotton/Dial Punlishers.

Gordon, R.E. and Gordon, K.K. (1957) 'Some social-psychiatric aspects of pregnancy and child bearing.' *Journal of the Medical Society of New Jersey 54*, 569–572.

Moll, L. (1920) 'Die Maternitätsneurose.' *Wiener Klinische Wochenschrift 33*, 160–162.

Oppenheim, H. (1919) *Ober Misopädie. Zeitschrift für die Gesamte Neurologie und Psychiatrie 45*, 1–18.

Sved-Williams, A.E. (1992) 'Phobic reactions of mothers to their own babies.' *Australian and New Zealand Journal of Psychiatry 142*, 238–246.

Tardieu, A. (1860) 'Étude medico-legale sûr les services et mauvais traitements exerces sûr des enfants.' *Annales d'Hygiene 15*, 361–398.

Index